The French in Algiers

The French in Algiers

Two Accounts of the Conflicts in North Africa During the 19th Century

The Soldier of the Foreign Legion

Clemens Lamping

The Prisoners of Abd-El-Kader

or,

Five Months' Captivity Among the Arabs

M. A. de France

Translated by Lady Duff Gordon

LEONAUR

The French in Algiers
Two Accounts of the Conflicts in North Africa During the 19th Century
by Clemens Lamping
and
M. A. de France
Translated by Lady Duff Gordon

First published under the titles
The French in Algiers

Leonaur is an imprint of Oakpast Ltd

ISBN: 978-0-85706-737-1 (hardcover)
ISBN: 978-0-85706-738-8 (softcover)

http://www.leonaur.com

Publisher's Notes

Contents

Preface   7

THE SOLDIER OF THE FOREIGN LEGION

Coleah   11

I join the Foreign Legion   23

The Foreign Legion   29

Algiers   40

March Through the Desert   46

The Prisoners   66

Hôpital du Dey   76

Voyage to Mostaganem   79

THE PRISONERS OF ABD-EL-KADER OR, FIVE MONTHS' CAPTIVITY AMONG THE ARABS

Painful Journey   91

Arrival at Abd-el-Kader's camp   98

Meurice's Story   103

French Deserters   109

The Beautiful Black Slave Girl   116

Horrible Execution of a Prisoner   123

Attempt to Convert Me   129

Marches   135

Offers of Exchange   142

Death of Meurice   150

Arrival at Algier   157

Preface

Clemens Lamping, the author of the first part of this little volume, is a young lieutenant in the Oldenburg service, who, tired of the monotonous life of a garrison, resigned his commission in July, 1839, and went to Spain to win his spurs under Espartero. Unfortunately he was detained by contrary winds, and arrived just as the treaty of Bergara had put an end to the war.

After spending six months at Madrid in abortive attempts to join the army in Arragon, then the seat of war, he resolved to go to Africa, and take part in the French crusade against the *infidels*. He accordingly went to Cadiz, encountering many adventures on his way through La Mancha and Andaluzia, and thence to Algiers, where he entered the foreign legion as a volunteer.

After two years of danger and hardship, the author returned to Oldenburg, having lost many illusions, and gained some experience. His sovereign restored him to his former grade in the service of Oldenburg, where he sits at his ease by his own fireside, and relates his adventures to his friends.

Lieutenant Lamping's *Reminiscences* are followed by the abridgement of a narrative of five months' captivity among the Arabs, by M. de France, a lieutenant in the French navy. The author modestly assures his readers that he is better skilled in the management of a ship than of his pen, and that his book would never have been published but at the request of his friends. It has nevertheless reached a second edition in France.

L. D. G.

'

The Soldier of the Foreign Legion

By Clemens Lamping

CHAPTER 1

Coleah

Coleah, September, 1841.

At last, my dear friend, after so many hardships and such various wanderings, I have leisure to write to you; and I have much, very much, to tell. The events of my life have lately followed each other in such rapid succession, that the dangers and sorrows of the noble, much-enduring Odysseus, nay, even the immortal adventures of the valiant Knight of La Mancha, are mere child's play in comparison with my own.

Since the month of April we have scarce had time to take breath; so rapidly did expedition follow expedition, and *razzia razzia*. The new Governor, Bugeaud, naturally enough wishes to show that he is equal to his post. His predecessor, Vallée, drew upon himself the imputation of indolence, but no one can deny to Bugeaud the possession of great energy and untiring activity. He encounters the Arabs with their own weapons, harassing them with incessant attacks, and burning and plundering the whole country. We have made two very important expeditions; the first against Thaza, a strong fortress belonging to Abd-el-Kader, situated on the borders of the desert. After destroying this place, we returned through the iron gates (*portes de fer*) to our own camp; this expedition occupied about four weeks.

A few days afterwards we started again to throw provisions into Milianah, and to lay waste the plains of the Chellif with fire and sword. It was exactly harvest time. In order to cut off from the Bedouins all means of existence, it was of course necessary to drive away their cattle and to burn their corn. Before long the whole plain looked like a sea of fire,

These expeditions, sent out in the very hottest season of the year, had such an effect upon the health of the soldiers, that the governor was compelled to allow them a short rest. The regiment to which I belonged had scarcely a third part fit for service, the other two-thirds were either dead or in the hospital. We were accordingly sent to Coleah to recruit our strength.

You will have a tolerably correct idea of our recruiting quarters when I tell you that one day is passed on guard, another in reconnoitring the enemy for several hours, and the third in working at the dry ditch (a sort of *pendant* to the great wall of China) intended to defend the plain of the Metidja against any sudden attacks of the Hadjutes. I assure you, however, that we think this life vastly agreeable, and consider ourselves as well off as if we were in Abraham's bosom. There was a time, indeed, when I should not have been quite so contented with my lot, but everything is relative in this best of all possible worlds.

Coleah is a true Arab town, which stands on the south-eastern declivity of the Sahel range of mountains, in a charming little nook, and is well supplied with water.

We are only twelve leagues from Algiers and about three from the sea, the proximity to which makes the place extremely healthy. The constant sea breeze renders the heat even of this season quite tolerable.

At our feet is stretched the vast plain of the Metidja bounded by the blue hills of the lesser Atlas range. We are quartered in a fortified camp outside the town, on a small eminence which commands it. Of course all the gates of the town and the market-place are guarded by our troops. My leisure hours, which, indeed, are not too many, are generally passed in sauntering about the streets.

The inhabitants of Coleah are pure descendants of the Moors, and still retain some traces of their former refinement; you must not confound them with the Bedouins and Kabyles, who always have been, and still are the lowest in point of civilisation. I have nowhere found the Arab so polished and so attractive as at Coleah, not even at Algiers and Oran; in those towns, their intercourse with the French has called forth all their rapacity, and spoiled the simplicity of their manners. It is a remarkable fact that in all these towns near the sea the Spanish language is still spoken, of course in a most corrupt dialect; a proof that some connection with Spain has constantly existed—often, no doubt, a very reluctant one on their parts: as in the reign of Charles V., who conquered great part of this coast.

To me this is very welcome, as it enables me to talk with the Arabs; it is not however easy to enter into conversation with them, as they are almost always silent and reserved towards strangers. In order to get them to talk it is necessary first to inspire confidence.

All my spare time is passed in the Arab coffee-house, the resort of the fashion and aristocracy of Coleah, and I have already succeeded in making some acquaintances. I have even obtained marks of evident goodwill from them by my earnest and sympathising attention to their singers and story-tellers, who never fail to attend the best coffee-houses.

The clerk of the *hakim* (the chief magistrate) is a great friend of mine. He is an exceedingly well-informed man, and with you he would be called "Mr. Secretary." He knows the whole *Koran* by heart, besides a host of Persian poems.

Like every man of sense he is exceedingly modest, lamenting his ignorance, and inquiring diligently into our European habits and manners. I have occasionally had the pleasure of seeing my friend Ben Jussuf (for that is his name) occupied in the fulfilment of his duties as clerk. Every Friday is kept by the Arabs as a holiday on which markets are held and judgments given. On this day the *hakim* sits in the public place before the great coffee-house, and holds his court; on his right hand stands his clerk who commits his judgments to paper, and on his left the executioner who inflicts the punishments awarded by the *hakim* on the spot.

This generally consists in some fifty or hundred strokes of the *bastinado*, and sometimes even in death; the latter, however, only for political offences, such as treasonable correspondence with the enemy, &c. Should the case be doubtful, the *hakim* orders a certain number of strokes of the *bastinado* to be given to both parties, and takes to himself the object of contention, generally a sheep or a donkey—a proceeding only differing from our own inasmuch as it has the great advantage of being more summary. If anyone is too profuse in his excuses, the *hakim* says to the executioner, "Give my comrade (among the Arabs every one is a comrade) some thirty strokes of the *bastinado*, to teach him not to confuse me any more with his ingenious evasions." In this country, you see, an advocate's fees would not be very high.

Coleah is held in great reverence by the Arabs as it contains Abd-el-Kader's vault, in which are deposited the bodies of several members of his family. The French have spared this tomb, in consideration of which Abd-el-Kader has vowed never to attack the town or its immediate neighbourhood.

The *hakim* belongs to the family of the *emir*, and is very rich: the

13

sheath and handle of his *yataghan* are of pure gold, and his horses the finest I ever saw. He is the ideal of a noble Arab—terrible to his enemies, hospitable and munificent to his friends, and especially charitable to the poor. I have seen him during the great fast, when the Mahomedans may eat nothing till after sunset, call together some thirty beggars every evening before his door, bring them food, and wait upon them himself with the help of his three grown up sons.

The beggars feasted upon *kuskussu* (porridge made with barley meal) and baked mutton with great dignity and grace; and when they were satisfied they rose, kissed the *hakim* on the shoulders and cheeks, and departed. The most contradictory qualities are often united in the Arab nature—harshness and benevolence, cruelty and generosity, rapacity and munificence: we should beware how we condemn them without further knowledge of their character, and we must on no account measure them by our Christian and European standard.

The great fast of the Mahomedans. which lasts forty days, began a few days ago. During all this time the Arabs eat nothing during the whole day, and are especially enjoined by the Prophet to be constant in devotion and to give freely to the poor:—and the Arab is a very strict observer of all his religious duties. Three times a day, at the hours of sunrise, mid-day, and sunset, the loud voice of the *marabout*, or priest, is heard from the minaret of the mosque summoning the faithful to prayer.

The moment the Arab hears the call of the *marabout* he throws himself upon the earth, wherever he may chance to be, and touches the ground with his brow, then rising again he stretches his arms toward heaven with his face turned in the direction of Mecca. His white flowing *bernouse* and his long beard give him a venerable and patriarchal air. Thus, surely, did Abraham, Isaac, and Jacob worship their God. The Arab has no hesitation in performing his devotions in the presence of the crowd, and is totally without either the false shame or the religious hypocrisy of an European.

Most Mahomedans wear a rosary of beads, which they tell while repeating sentences out of the *Koran*; to this is usually appended a large brass comb, with which they comb their beards during their orisons with the most solemn earnestness. The impression produced by this on Europeans is highly comical, but to the Mahomedan it seems natural enough, as any purification of the body, such as combing and washing, are to him in themselves religious acts.

They are by no means behind us in superstition, and frequently hang, as an amulet round the neck of a favourite horse, a leathern bag containing some verses out of the *Koran*, to protect them from evil machinations.

The Arab is great and admirable at the hour of death. I have seen many Arabs die, but never did I see one beg his life or utter any unmanly complaint. when his hour is come he recommends his soul to Mahomed, and dies.

They have physicians only for external injuries or for fevers incidental to the climate: when one of them is attacked by an internal disorder or by the decrepitude of age, his relations quietly leave him to his fate, and no one troubles his head about him again.

It was but a few days ago that I saw an Arab die thus on the threshold of his own house: he had already lain there some days with his *bernouse* drawn over his head. When he felt the approach of death he exclaimed with a loud voice, "Mahomed! Mahomed!" and died.

The burial is conducted much in the same manner as with us. The corpse, rolled in a mantle, and with the face uncovered, is borne to the grave by four men. The priest who walks before it sings a song to which the others respond in chorus: but their song is cheerful, and their step quick; for the departed has quitted the hardships and sorrows of this life, and now rests in Paradise beside a shady fountain, served by women whose beauty is unfading.

After the corpse has been lowered into it, the tomb is carefully bricked up, in order to prevent the jackals and hyenas from scratching up the body. The mourners then sit round the grave, and one of the near relations of the deceased gives to everyone present a piece of bread and some fruit.

The fair sex is not altogether fair here, at least in my opinion. No one can deny that the Arab women have graceful figures and regular features, but they want those essential requisites of beauty—a soul and individual expression. They are all exactly alike, and their faces express but two passions—love and hate; all nicer shades of feeling are wanting. How, indeed, would it be possible for them to acquire intellectual or bodily cultivation, when the greater part of their time is spent seated cross-legged grinding corn in a hand-mill, or asleep?

The married women are seldom seen out of their houses, and then only closely veiled. The young girls, on the contrary, are to be found every morning at sunrise outside the gate of the town, standing by the fountain, at which they assemble with stone jars on their shoulders, to fetch water for the day's consumption. This truly Eastern scene calls to mind Rebecca at the well, drawing water for her father's flocks.

If a stranger asks a daughter of the town to give him a draught of water (*alma*), the maiden readies him the jar with a kindly nod; but when he has slaked his thirst she pours away the remainder and draws fresh water, for the lips of the infidel have polluted it.

The Arab women wear a white woollen garment confined under the breast by a girdle, and a white cloth twisted round the head. Their ornaments generally consist in rings in their ears and on their ankles, which are invariably naked. One cannot deny the efficiency of this graceful manner of calling attention to the beauty of their feet, which are truly exquisite. These rings, among women of the lower class, are of silver; among those of the higher class (and here, as in every other country, there are distinctions of class), they are of gold.

A few days ago my friend Ben Jussuf invited me to go with him to his house. I, of course, seized with joy this opportunity of seeing him in his domestic circle.

He knocked at the door, which is invariably kept shut by day and by night in all Arab houses, a woman shortly appeared and inquired who was there; at Ben Jussuf's answer the door was opened, but when the woman saw me with her husband she instantly concealed her face, and was about to run away; my friend, however, commanded her to remain. She was his wife, and besides her he had two others, who were seated cross-legged in the court, one of them grinding corn in a hand-mill, the other combing the hair of a boy about five or six years old. I should have guessed them all three to be at least forty, but Ben Jussuf assured me that they were all under five-and-twenty; their faces and figures were withered, and the bloom of youth quite gone, their eyes alone still retained their fire. At twenty the Arab women begin to fade, and at thirty they are old matrons.

They all seemed to live in perfect harmony, and the manner of the women towards their lord and master was obliging even to servility. To judge by appearances, it must be easier to keep house with three wives than with one; perhaps the rule "*divide et impera*" holds good in love as well as in politics, I must however confess that I do not envy the Mahomedan gentlemen their frigid joys, nor do they seem to find much satisfaction in them themselves.

The women here are mere slaves; of that chivalrous homage paid by the Spanish Moors to their women no traces are left save in the songs and poems of the Arabs.

The children are educated by women up to their seventh year; on reaching that age the boy is put in possession of a *bernouse* and a pony, and is no longer allowed to eat with the women; should his father be away he has supreme authority over the whole household, not excepting his own mother.

The manner of arranging a marriage is very simple among the Arabs. A man takes a sum of money or any article of value, and offers it to whomsoever he happens to meet with, saying, "Comrade! I hear you have a marriageable daughter, give her to me as a wife, and take this as a marriage gift." If the other thinks the match a suitable one, he replies, "Yes: here she is, take her with you;" and the marriage is concluded. The father must, however, warrant her to be a maid; and if the husband finds she is not, he takes her home next morning and demands his present back again.

Yesterday we made one of the most interesting reconnoitring expeditions in which I have been engaged. These expeditions occupy several hours, and are undertaken for the purpose of driving the Hadjutes out of the *rayons* of the blockhouses, and the gardens belonging to the town. The Hadjutes inhabit the Sahel mountains to the westward of Coleah, and are notoriously the most thievish set of fellows in all Africa. They are the people who, on the 1st of May, cut off the heads of about forty of our regiment at Delhi Ibrahim.

We set out before sunrise, and marched down towards the Metidja. I was detached on one side with a dozen others, to search the thicket with which all this country is covered. We followed a track trodden by wild boasts, for a human foot rarely wanders in this place. We suddenly emerged into an open space of about thirty square feet, and as we stepped out of the thicket a large panther stood before us, at about twenty feet distance, and gazed at us with a look of mingled wonder and indignation as though he would say, "What seek ye in my kingdom?"

We, however, appealed to the right of the strongest— two or three muskets were instantly levelled and discharged at him, but with one bound the panther disappeared among the bushes. A ball or two must have reached him, but if they do not happen to hit him on the head, which is his only tender point, he takes no heed of them. These beasts, and still more hyenas and jackals, abound in this district, as is shown from the ridiculously small price which is asked by the Arabs for the skins of these animals.

The Arab chiefs consider the skin of the tiger and the panther as one of their principal ornaments. The head of the animal is generally fastened to the saddle-bow, (the head and teeth are essential,) and the skin waves to and fro with every motion of the horse, so that at a distance one might almost imagine that some wild beast had just taken a deadly spring upon the rider.

But to return to my reconnoitring expedition. On coming near the plain we turned westward, to pass the gorge in which Coleah lies. As there is no lack of water here, the most abundant vegetation prevails, and we were delighted and astonished at the extreme richness of the scene. The luxuriant aloe sends up its blossoms to a height of twenty feet, and a species of sedgy rush grows as high as a moderate house.

From thence we turned towards our dry ditch, which is nearly finished, and climbed past it up to the very top of the chain of mountains, from whence the sea is visible. Here we found plenty of fruit trees, on some of which the fruit was quite ripe; the pomegranates and the figs were delicious. In this spot the commander ordered his troops to halt. After the necessary precautions had been taken, we were allowed to gather the fruit, and were soon scattered about the gardens in all directions, filling our *shackos* and pocket handkerchiefs.

After plucking some fine pomegranates, I lay down under a shady pomegranate tree, and looked out over the sea.

I could clearly discern on the blue surface of the sea a ship whose prow was directed towards Europe, and whose sails were filled by a favourable breeze; the thought involuntarily occurred to me, "Would I were on board that ship, sailing towards my own home." This indeed looks a little like home-sickness, but I know not why anyone should be ashamed of the feeling. Even Odysseus, the wisest of mortals, was not ashamed to weep aloud, and to long after his paternal hearth, his wife, and his child; and why should not I—who am the least wise of men—honestly confess that there are moments when I also long for those who are dear to me? Besides, I have seen nearly all there is to see in Algeria, the future can but be a repetition of the past.

I was on the point of beginning a touching monologue—a failing I have long been subject to—when I was startled out of my dreams by several shots, and a cry of "*Aux armes! Aux armes!*" We all ran to our muskets, and were ready in a moment, but the alarm proved a false one. Some twenty Hadjutes, who were lying in ambuscade behind a neighbouring hill, had fired several shots at our sentinels, who thought a considerable force must be concealed there. But the moment we showed ourselves the Hadjutes fled towards the open country, chased by a squadron of our horse: the Arabs, however, got clear off, and the only damage done was to my monologue, and to the ripe pomegranates which I threw away in the hurry and confusion. It was not till about nine o'clock, just before the oppressive heat of the day, that we returned to Coleah.

The chief wealth of the inhabitants of this town consists in large herds of cattle and fruit-tree gardens; it is surrounded by the most magnificent fruit trees as far as the eye can reach. The figs and pomegranates are now ripe, and we feast on them luxuriously. I say we, for the most complete community of goods prevails among the Arabs and ourselves. The soldier and the beggar are born communists. I must say, however, that the Arabs do not seem much to relish this same communism, for we have several times missed some of our soldiers; it is true we found them again in the gardens, but without their heads.

The fruit here is at times extremely dangerous to the head, and when eaten immoderately, it is equally injurious to the stomach; this is particularly the case with the figs which produce violent thirst, and if this is allayed with draughts of water fever and diarrhoea are the inevitable consequences. The fig trees bear fruit three times a year, but one of the crops is usually of inferior quality: the natives generally gather this crop and press it into large cakes; when dry these are exceedingly wholesome, and form, throughout the year, a favourite dish at the Arab's table. The pomegranate is a delicious fruit, and much less unwholesome. The oranges are so wholesome that any one may eat twenty a day with impunity. Unfortunately it is not till November that they are ripe.

The wild laurel grows in great quantities near the town, and attains a very considerable height; I can boast of having tasted the fruit of the laurel as well as its leaf. It is about the size of a strawberry and very sweet. The sight of a laurel tree always recalls to my mind that noble Roman folded in his imperial mantle, with the laurel wreathed round his bald head. Time was when I would have given the last drop of my blood for but one leaf from this same laurel wreath; but I have now begun to perceive that when one is no emperor but a mere corporal of *voltigeurs* the laurel is only good in soup.

All Arabs of any education or wealth assemble at the coffee-house. To them it supplies the place of theatres and concerts, balls and tea-parties. There they spend the whole day, sometimes staying till past midnight. The coffee-house, like almost all other houses in the south, is built round a square court paved with white marble, in the middle of which plays a fountain. Round the court are two rows of pillars supporting the women's apartments; the rooms all look into the court: on the outside nothing is to be seen but high dismal walls, for the Arab does not choose that inquisitive eyes should peer into his holy of holies.

The vine or ivy is generally trained up the house so as to shade the whole court, and keep out the oppressive rays of the sun. Under this natural arcade the sons of Ishmael sit on soft carpets lazily splashing with their naked feet in the water which flows from the fountain over the marble floor.

Here they imbibe coffee, sherbet, songs, and tales: in short, it is a foretaste of Paradise. The coffee is not bad, only that they drink it black and have the bad taste to reckon the grounds the best part of the coffee. Before the slave hands one the cup, he stirs it with a reed for fear the dregs should sink to the bottom.

The Arab is a passionate lover of music and poetry: the coffee-houses are, therefore, never without their poets and storytellers. Their songs are monotonous, and they accompany them with the *mandoline*, as in Andalusia. Coleah possesses the best story-teller and singer in all Africa, so celebrated for the melody of his voice as to be called the second Hafiz.

I must confess that fame has not said too much in his favour. His name is Sofi; at the age of thirteen he had the misfortune to lose a leg in an encounter with the Hadjutes, and since that time he has devoted himself entirely to singing and poetry. I never saw an Arab whose countenance wore so noble an expression, or whose features so clearly reflected the feelings of his soul. He does not usually come to the coffee-house till after sunset: as soon as he is seated the Arabs place themselves in a half-circle round him, with their eyes attentively fixed upon him. After striking a few notes on the *mandoline*, he began one day to recite a ballad of the great deeds and of the downfall of the Moorish kings.

It was always the same measure, the same tune, sung now in a louder, now in a lower tone, and one would have expected its monotony to weary the hearers: but not so; the longer one listened, the more fascinating it became. First he sang the conquest of Spain, the Battle of Xeres, and the death of Don Rodrigo. He then struck the cords of the *mandoline* more loudly, and sang the victories of Abd-el-Rahman, and the pomp and glory of Cordova, till the eyes of his hearers glistened. By slow degrees the notes became softer, and his voice trembled as he sang the death of the Abencerrages, and the shameful flight of Boabdil, the last king of Granada. The sounds of his *mandoline* died away, the Arabs hung their heads upon their breasts, and the pipes fell from their hands.

The unfeigned grief of the Moors touched me to the heart. I told my friend Ben Jussuf, who sat next to me, that I had visited the scenes of their former greatness, the palace of their kings—the Alhambra, and the mosque of Cordova, the Kaaba of the west.

Scarcely had he told this to the others, when they crowded round me begging me to tell all I had seen, and I thus became an involuntary storyteller, with Ben Jussuf for my interpreter. I gave them an account of the grandeur and beauty of the mosque of Cordova, its thirteen hundred columns, and the tombs of their kings. I described to them the Alhambra, the marble lions who keep watch at the palace gates, the splendid hall where the Abencerrages held their feasts, and where they were barbarously murdered. I told them that I myself had seen the traces of their noble blood which time itself had been unable to efface from the polished marble floor.

Overcome by the remembrance of the tragical fate of their most heroic race, the Arabs covered their faces with their *bernouses*. "Young man." said the *hakim*, kissing my forehead. "thank the Prophet that he hath vouchsafed to thee the sight of these marvels."

After a pause the *hakim* said, "Friend Sofi, know you not some pleasant story which may dissipate the melancholy of our comrades, who still sit with drooping heads?" and Sofi, without further entreaty, began the following tale.

Far beyond Milianah, on the banks of the Mina, there once lived an *emir*, on whom *Allah* had bestowed every blessing. His life was pure and blameless. He gave the fourth part of all he possessed to the poor, and the hour of prayer was more welcome to him than the hour of feasting. This *emir*, whose name was Abubekr, had a mare which he loved above all other things; she was white, without spot or blemish, and more swift than the wind of the desert, and she could travel for three days without drinking a single drop of water.

One evening before sunset, Abubekr stood by the brook cleaning his favourite mare. He washed her neck and her haunches, addressing her by the most endearing names, and the mare looked in his face with her soft expressive eyes as though she understood every word he said. At this moment the *marabout* called the hour of prayer from the minaret, but Abubekr heard him not. At last the sun sank down behind mount Atlas, and the *emir* knew that the hour of prayer was past. In despair he cast himself upon the ground and cried, 'Woe is me, I have forgotten thee, O Lord the creator, for the creature; have mercy upon me, and graciously accept this sacrifice as a token of my repentance.'

Having said this, he took his spear and plunged it into the breast of his mare, and she fell to the earth and died. Sorrowful, but conscious of having done aright, Abubekr returned to his dwelling, folded his *bernouse* about him, and slept. And *Allah* appeared to him in a dream and spake to him thus, 'Abubekr, I have proved thy heart, and have seen that thou walkest before me justly. I desire not the sacrifices of the just, but their good deeds, for I am gracious. Arise, thy mare liveth.' The *emir* started up rejoicing and hastened to the door—there steed his darling mare, and neighed joyfully at the sight of him. Abubekr prostrated himself and touched the dust with his forehead, exclaiming, '*Allah*, thy wisdom is infinite, but thy mercy is yet greater than thy wisdom!'

Farewell. Next week our regiment will march to Algiers, whence it will embark for Oran.

This letter is accompanied by a brief account of my adventures from the day on which I landed in Africa until now.

CHAPTER 2

I join the Foreign Legion

Mustapha Superieur, August, 1840.

We came in sight of the coast of Africa on the 8th of August at nine in the morning. This was the second time I had seen it: the first was in the straits of Gibraltar. But I now beheld it with far different feelings. I was about to tread the land of the Bedouin and of the Kabyle in the full enjoyment of my strength and liberty—perhaps never to return.

The first step in life is a man's own choice, the second is no longer within his control but subject to foreign and often hostile influences.

You may well shake your head, dear friend, reproach me as usual with Quixotism, and wonder how it is that the experience gained in Spain has not cooled my ardour. I allow it is cooled, but not chilled. I have still ardour enough left to venture—a true Don Quixote of the nineteenth century—a crusade for civilisation and freedom. Forward, then, and let me pass the Rubicon, without hesitation.

The steamboat strove onwards with might and main, the coast rose higher out of the sea every moment, and before very long the glorious bay in which lies Algiers, and the Sahel range of mountains lay clear before us. The town itself is built in the shape of an amphitheatre on the declivity of the Sahel hills, and when seen from a distance looks like a huge white pyramid, for the town forms a triangle the highest point of which is crowned by the Casabah—the former residence of the *Dey*. The bay presents an enchanting: scene for a few miles eastward of Algiers. The sides of the mountains are crowded with beautiful gardens and villas built in the noble Moorish style.

On the very ridge of the Sahel is a semicircular chain of fortified camps and blockhouses intended to protect this fruitful district against the inroads of the Berbers. The harbour is so small that only a few ships can ride there, and the greater part are compelled to lie at anchor outside in the roads. We had scarce dropped one anchor then a number of small boats surrounded the ship to convey us ashore, the rowers were galley slaves who, in a melancholy air, kept time to the stroke of their oars. The subject of the song was as follows:—

An aged galley slave, with the faded ribbon of the legion of honour on his breast, stands on the pier and looks gloomily down upon the sea as though he would fathom its depths with his chains. A marshal of France passes by and sees the ribbon on his breast. 'Where,' he asks, 'did you deserve it?' The slave answers gloomily, 'I won it in such a battle;' and the marshal recognises the man who once saved his life. Filled with gratitude, he entreats the pardon of the king for the unhappy prisoner, and it is granted.

This song made an indelible impression on my mind, and convinced me that even the galleys have a poetry of their own.

The lower part of the town which surrounds the port has already acquired a completely European character. The streets of Babazoun and of the Marine are as handsome and as elegant as the *boulevards* of Paris. The upper town retains its Arab colour, and is exclusively inhabited by Moors and Jews. The streets are so narrow that it is with difficulty that two horses can pass in them; and the Arabs have no kind of carriages. I was beyond measure surprised at the motley crowd with which I suddenly found myself surrounded, and fancied that I must be in a masquerade; Arabs and Frenchmen, Jews and Italians, Spaniards and Negroes were mixed in picturesque confusion.

Next door to an elegant French milliner, an Arab barber was shaving the heads of his fellow-countrymen, and an Italian *restaurant*, who extolled his macaroni to every passer-by, was the neighbour of a Moorish slipper-maker. Everything wore a martial aspect, troops were landing, and horse-soldiers galloping about the streets; in short, I soon perceived that the gay scene around me was no carnival merry-making.

In order to get rid of the uncomfortable feelings left by a sea voyage I wished to take a bath, and asked the first man I met where one was to be found. A good-natured, talkative Frenchman pointed out a Moorish bath to me in the very next street and on my way thither told me his whole life and adventures, *en passant*, which I have been so fortunate as to forget. The bath was excellent, and cost only one *franc* from first to last. After bathing me for some time in lukewarm water, a couple of sturdy Arabs scrubbed me with brushes and kneaded me with their fists in such a manner that I expected the fellows would break every bone in my body. They next rubbed me with perfumed oil, wrapped me in a *bernouse*, and gave me a cup of black coffee and a pipe; the latter was lost upon me, as I do not smoke. I departed feeling like one newly born, and resumed my ramble about the streets.

After wandering about for some time without any settled purpose, I began to feel a certain longing after I knew not what, an inward yearning which I would fain have satisfied; at last, just as I was passing the shop of an Italian *restaurant* which sent forth a most seductive odour of fried fish, the happy thought struck me that I perhaps was hungry. I accordingly went in and ordered a dish of fish, which made their appearance very well fried in oil, and a bottle of Spanish wine. My sensations were soon so agreeable that I forgot all my good and evil fortunes, nay, almost even the reason of my presence here. As the *restaurant*, a Neapolitan, also let lodgings, I hired a room there for a few days, to reconnoitre the ground a little before taking any further steps.

After having satisfied my curiosity for the present with looking at this strange scene, I went out at the gate Babazoun (Eastern gate) towards Mustapha Superieur, which was formerly the palace of the *Dey's* son, but now serves for a *depôt* of the Foreign Legion. It is built on a declivity of the Sahel, about a league from Algiers, and is surrounded by most exquisite fruit gardens. Traces of the former splendour of this palace still remained, notwithstanding the ravages of the soldiery. It is built round two large courts, the smaller of which is adorned with sixty-four marble columns supporting most splendid rooms, which were formerly inhabited by the prince's *seraglio*, but are now turned into workshops for a whole company of shoemakers and tailors.

As soon as possible I presented myself before General Von Hulsen, who commanded the Foreign Legion, and related my former life to him. After quietly listening to my story and my determination to enter the Legion as a volunteer, he plainly told me that I was about to commit a great piece of folly and to sacrifice my health and life to no purpose. His words have proved but too true; but, unfortunately, I am not one of those who can profit by the experience of others: I must see everything with my own eyes and touch everything with my own hands. The general, seeing that I was determined to stay, promised to protect me as far as lay in his power.

Unfortunately he was killed three months after, while we were throwing provisions into Fonduk: far too soon for me and for the Legion. He belonged to the Pomeranian family Von Hulsen, and had served in the French army under Napoleon.

Hulsen's was a true German character, bold and straightforward even to roughness; he was the only one who had the courage to protect the interests of the Foreign Legion against the French general officers.

I was asked whether I knew how to load and fire, and on my replying in the affirmative, I was, without further question, transferred to the third battalion of the Legion, at that moment quartered at Dschigeli, for which spot a transport was to sail in a few days. Until then I was my own master, and employed these few, and possibly last hours of liberty in strolling about the town and the surrounding country to satisfy my curiosity. Although these were the hottest and most unhealthy months of the year, I did not find the heat nearly so oppressive as I had expected. The whole northern declivity of the Sahel mountains enjoys a temperate and agreeable climate, owing to its proximity to the sea. We hear of scarcely any illness here.

The whole coast, from Algiers as far as the fortified camp of Kouba, was formerly inhabited by the most wealthy Turks and Moors, who spent here in Oriental ease and voluptuous idleness the riches they obtained by piracy. Their country houses, built in a noble style of Moorish architecture, are proofs of the wealth of their former possessors. These are still in good repair, (as at time of first publication), and are inhabited by Frenchmen and Spaniards who have bought them for a trifle for the sake of the gardens of fruit and vegetables. The soil is wonderfully productive owing to the numerous springs which rise in the mountains and water the ground throughout the year. Traces are still found both of the Roman and the Moorish method of irrigation.

The bold arches of the Romans have long since fallen to decay, while the modest and simple earthen pipes of the Moors, which creep below the surface of the earth, still convey a fresh and plentiful supply of water. These few square miles on the Sahel form nearly the whole of the boasted French colony in Africa; *cafés* and canteens are their only possessions beyond the fortified camps and the range of the blockhouses, even near the largest towns, such as Medeah, Milianah, Mascara, &c., and these are only supported by the military, and may therefore be said to draw their resources from France.

During the first years of the French occupation a considerable tract of the plains of Metidja came under cultivation. But the bad policy and worse system of defence of the French soon ruined the colonists. One morning, in the year 1839, Abd-el-Kader and his hordes poured down from the lesser Atlas range and destroyed everything with fire and sword. Those who escaped death were dragged into captivity. Since then the colonists have lost all confidence in the Government, and it will be very long before they recover it.

Agriculture requires perfect security of property and, above all, personal security. Setting aside the precarious condition of the colonists, the French are thoroughly bad settlers, and only know how to set up *cafés*. The few good agriculturists to be found here are either Germans or Spaniards. It is remarkable that the Spaniards, who in their own country are so lazy that they had rather starve than work, are here the very best agricultural labourers. Their diligence and economy almost amount to avarice.

My favourite walk is to the Plane Tree Café, so called from a group of beautiful plane trees which overshadow it. A plentiful spring of water gushes out of a rock close by, and tumbles down the hill on its way to the sea; so that nothing is wanting to the enjoyment of an inhabitant of the south. The house stands under Mustapha Superieur and affords a magnificent view over the sea and the bay of Algiers. On this spot some dozen Turks and Arabs dream away the greater part of their lives. The owner of the *café* is an old Turk who formerly served among the *mamelukes* of the *Dey*. He parsed some years of his life a prisoner in Spain, where, besides corrupt and broken Spanish, he learned to drink and swear. It was comical enough to hear this "malignant and turbaned Turk" introduce a *caramba* between every other word. He told me some very remarkable facts relating to the *Dey's* government. It seems that the tribes could only be kept in any obedience by means of a strong body of cavalry continually scouring the country.

Whenever a tribe delayed the payment of its tribute the mamelukes came down upon them in the dead of the night, cut down all the men and carried off the women and cattle. He was by no means satisfied with the French mode of warfare and maintained that they ought to have more cavalry, and that the infantry, for which he entertained a profound contempt, were far too slow in their movements. "The first thing in war," said he, with a volley of Spanish oaths, "is quickness: the French always arrive too late." You see that my friend the Turk is a very distinguished strategist; and I almost think it must have been from him that Bugeaud afterwards took the hint of the *razzia* and the *colonne mobile*.

The old greybeard is a devoted admirer of Spanish women and Spanish wine; when talking of either his eyes sparkled. He generally kept a keg of *Malaga* hidden in his house and took a good pull at it from time to time. When in a good humour he gave me a wink and we drank to the health of the Spanish women. He thoroughly despised his Arab guests, whom he called "*brutos*" (beasts), who were fit for nothing but to count their beads and smoke their pipes.

You perceive that my friend Hassan is a freethinker, who has shaken off all the restraints of the *Koran*. Had the Arabs suspected this but for a moment, they would have spat in his face, and never set foot over his threshold again; for they are strict observers of their religious duties.

As we are under orders to start at a moment's notice for Dschigeli, I took leave of the Turk yesterday. He gave me his blessing and a glass of *Malaga*, recommending me, above all things not to trust those dogs of Arabs, and to beware of eating figs and drinking water.

Tomorrow we embark on board a steamer bound for Bona.

CHAPTER 3

The Foreign Legion

Dschigeli, August, 25.

We reached Dschigeli on the 15th, after a most prosperous voyage of thirty-six hours, which included a short stay at Budschia.

During the summer the surface of the Mediterranean is almost always as smooth as a mirror. The blue transparent water looks so gentle and harmless that one can scarce believe in the terrific powers which slumber in its bosom. In the later autumn it entirely alters its character; storms, and frequently even hurricanes, render the African coasts the most dangerous in the world; the more so, since the whole territory occupied by the French does not contain a single safe and capacious harbour of refuge. Last year, the French lost in the roads before Stora, a short distance from hence, no less than forty vessels in one night.

The government has endeavoured to remedy this evil by constructing artificial harbours, and has, at an enormous cost, somewhat enlarged that of Algiers by sinking blocks of stone and a species of cement into the sea; but of course little can be effected in this manner.

Dschigeli, which also has only a small roadstead, is built on a rock rising out of the sea; it belongs to the province of Constantina and lies between Budschia and Philippeville. It is inhabited by Turks and Arabs, who formerly drove a thriving trade in piracy. Although the town looks like a mere heap of stones, it is said still to contain much hidden treasure. The soldiers are already hoping for an outbreak among the population which may afford them an excuse for pillaging the town. This does not, however, seem very likely, as the Arabs are on very good terms with the garrison, and not without reason, for the Kabyles who dwell in the neighbouring mountains would not treat them so well as the French do.

The whole district between Algiers and Dschigeli, along which runs the high range of the Aphronne mountains, is the proper country of the Kabyles.

The French possess no more of it than what they have enclosed within a line of blockhouses, that is, about half a square mile. Our battalion, the third of the Foreign Legion, forms the whole garrison: it is commanded by Lieutenant-Colonel Picolou, a Frenchman. Like the rest of the Legion, this battalion is composed of men of all nations and all ranks: Spaniards and Italians, Germans and Belgians, Dutchmen and Poles, only no English. Most of them have joined the service out of mere folly, some from political or civil offences, and a few from misfortune.

These men are for the most part brutal and undisciplined, but ready to encounter anything. They form a band who, under an energetic leader, might do great things. Like all hirelings, our corps has much of the character of Wallenstein's camp. At first I thought that my fate was a very tragical one, but even this comfort was soon taken from me. There is not one among us who has not the history and adventures of his life to tell, and the worst of all is that one is forced to confess that there is nothing tragical which has not its comic side. I may safely assert that I have heard more biographies in one day here than are to be found in all Plutarch.

Nearly all the commissions in the Legion are held by French men who look upon this as a short cut to advancement. Among the officers are also a few Poles and Swiss; the latter of whom have joined the service since the revolution of July. But, in general, it is very difficult for a foreigner to attain to the rank of an officer.

Although Dschigeli lies under nearly the same latitude as Algiers. it is far hotter and more unhealthy. Nearly half the garrison is rendered unfit for service by fever, which makes the duty of those who are well doubly severe. The oppressive heat has a very remarkable effect upon all newcomers, whose strength leaves them from day to day; and men, as strong as lions before, creep about with pale yellow faces and with voices as small as those of children. Every morning before daybreak seven or eight corpses are secretly carried out of the town.

Hitherto I have resisted the influence of the climate, but I take more care of myself than the rest, and do not indulge in eating fruit, &c. The first rule of health is to follow as nearly as possible the manner of life of the natives of foreign countries, for one may fairly presume that they have good reasons for adhering to particular customs from generation to generation. Most inhabitants of the north of Europe ruin their health by persisting in the same habits abroad which they follow in their own country.

September, 1840.

We spend alternately fourteen days in the town, and fourteen in the blockhouses: the latter is by far the most interesting. The block-houses, placed in a semicircle on the heights surrounding .he town, are built of oak planks imported from France and of sufficient thickness to turn a bullet. They are generally two stories high, and are protected by a wall and a ditch. The largest are provided with two cannons and some wall-pieces, which are of great service.

To prevent time from hanging heavy on our hands, our friends the Kabyles come down from the neighbouring mountains to pay their respects to us. They greet us from afar with a torrent of friendly epithets, such as *"hahluf"* (swine), &c., which is quickly followed by a shower of balls. We are no less civil in our turn, allowing them to approach within a short distance, when we treat them to a volley of musketry and a few discharges from the fieldpieces; whereupon they usually retire somewhat tranquillized but still vehement in abuse. We of course have much the best of it behind our walls and ditches, but from time to time some of us are wounded or killed.

A few days ago they attacked us with unusual fury and pertinac-ity. Some time before sunrise we saw a large party of Kabyles coin-ing down from the mountains: as far as the eve could reach the place swarmed with white *bernouses*. Every blockhouse was attacked at the same moment. Our well-directed fire was insufficient to keep off an enemy which pressed upon us in dense masses, and in a moment they were close under the walls. Here they could no longer do us any dam-age with their shots; but in their rage they threw huge stones over the walls upon our heads. We made a rapid retreat into our blockhouses and *barricadoed* the doors. In one moment the Kabyles climbed the outer walls, and attempted in their blind fury to storm the block-houses. Some of them tried, but in vain, to throw the cannon over the walls; and they now had the worst of the fight.

The half of our party who were in the upper story removed a plank which was left loose for the purpose, and poured their fire down upon the heads of the Kabyles, while some cannoneers who were with us threw a number of hand-grenades, of which we had good store, among them. This was rather more than they could bear, and they dispersed in all directions, yelling fearfully; they however carried off their dead and wounded, for the Mohamedan never leaves his comrades in the hands of the foe. They did not repeat their visit for several days after this. The Kabyles, who are a strong and courageous race, inhabit fixed dwellings, and employ themselves in agriculture as well as in cattle-breeding. They always fight on foot, armed with a *yataghan* and a long rifle which will carry almost as far as our wall-pieces.

They hardly ever attack by night, for one of the precepts of the *Koran* is—neither to wander nor to wage war by night, and this they pretty scrupulously obey; and indeed they are altogether far better Mohamedans than we are Christians.

I need not add that on these occasions everyone does his duty, for each fights for that which he most values, namely his head. He who falls into the hands of the Kabyles is born under no lucky planet—his head is instantly cut off and borne away as a trophy.

The commandant marched up into the mountains one night with the whole garrison, to chastise the Kabyles for their insolence. We started at midnight under the guidance of some Arabs who knew the country and marched, without stopping and in deep silence, uphill and down dale until just before daybreak, when the crowing of cocks and the baying of dogs gave us notice that we were close upon a tribe. We were ordered to halt, and two companies with a few field-pieces were left behind on an eminence.

After a short rest we started again, and the first glimmer of light showed the huts of the tribe straight before us. An old Kabyle was at that moment going out with a pair of oxen to plough; as soon as he saw us he uttered a fearful howl and fled, but a few well-directed shots brought him down. In one moment the grenadiers and *voltigeurs*, who were in advance, broke through the hedge of prickly pear which generally surrounds a Kabyle village, and the massacre began. Strict orders had been given to kill all the men and only to take the women and children prisoners: for we followed the precept of "an eye for an eye, a tooth for a tooth."

A few men only reeled half awake out of their huts, In it most of them still lay fast asleep; not one escaped death. The women and children rushed, howling and screaming, out of their burning huts in time to see their husbands and brothers butchered. One young woman with an infant at her breast started back at the sight of strange men exclaiming "Mohamed! Mohamed!" and ran into her burning hut. Some soldiers sprang forward to save her, but the roof had already fallen in and she and her child perished in the flames.

We then returned with our booty, and it was high time, for other tribes of Kabyles came flocking together from every side, attracted by the noise. We were forced to retreat in such haste that we left the greater part of the cattle behind. The fire of the companies we had stationed in our rear with the fieldpieces at last gained us time to breathe. We however had but few killed and wounded.

A few days after, a deputation was sent by the survivors with proposals for the exchange of the women and children against cattle, which was accepted. It is a point of honour with the Kabyles not to leave their women and children in the enemies' hands. They most conscientiously ransomed even the old women whom we would willingly have given them *gratis*.

For several days we have been suffering severely from the wind of the desert (*samoom*) which prevails here during the months of August and September. This wind is scorching and impregnated with minute particles of sand. At its approach all are filled with terror, large drops of sweat stand on one's brow, and the only means of escape is to lie flat on one's face and to hold one's breath. Those who inhale the air die in twenty minutes.

Fortunately the *samoom* only lasts from a quarter of an hour to twenty minutes, but it returns several times a day. During its prevalence all hostilities cease; for the natives and the very wild beasts are subject to its influence. When surprised by this wind during a march, all instantly halt. Camels, horses, and mules, instinctively turn their backs to the wind and hold their noses close to the ground until the danger is past.

The day before yesterday we had a hot encounter with the Kabyles, after a fashion truly Homeric, in defence of our oxen. Our company was ordered to escort the cattle, which are numerous, to the water.

The incessant heat had already dried up all the fountains and springs within the line of the blockhouses, so that we were forced to drive the cattle beyond it to a stream which flows from the mountains and never fails. We advanced as usual *en tirailleurs* to cover the watering-place, but we had scarcely reached the further side of the stream when we were greeted on all sides by yells and bullets. The Kabyles had hidden themselves in the brushwood close by, and occupied an eminence opposite to us. In order to make use of our strongest weapon, the bayonet, which is much dreaded by the Kabyles, we advanced up the hill with levelled bayonets and took it at the first attack. But scarce had we reached the top when we received a heavy fire from all sides, the Kabyles having surrounded us in a semicircle. In a moment we had several killed and wounded and were forced to retreat faster than we had advanced, the Kabyles pressing furiously on our rear. The commanding officer exclaimed: "*Sauvez les blesses! Sauvez les blesses!*"

A non-commissioned officer close beside me had been shot through the jaw; he had completely lost his senses, and was reeling round and round like a drunken man. I seized him under the arm and dragged him towards the nearest blockhouse into which the company retreated. We were the very last, and the Kabyles yelled wildly close behind us while their bullets whistled in our ears; I was not hit however, and succeeded in bringing my charge safely home, conscious of having done my duty as a soldier and as a man. We had but just reached the blockhouse when the *Commandant Superieur* came up with a reinforcement of several companies, and sent us all out again to rescue the cattle, which by this time had all but fallen into the enemy's hands. The beasts were so deeply engaged in the noble occupation of drinking that it was almost impossible to move them from the spot.

We now repulsed the Kabyles, and at length the horsemen succeeded in driving off the cattle. After this we came to a sort of tacit understanding with the enemy to leave each other in peace at the stream, for they too had to water their cattle there and might have been seriously incommoded by us from the blockhouse.

This was my first battle in the open field, and I cannot say that it made much impression upon me. My imagination had pictured the terrors of the scene so vividly to me that the reality fell far short of it. I was moreover prepared for it by all manner of perils which I had encountered by land and by sea. I have frequently observed that men of lively imagination (and accordingly most southerns) have a greater dread of fancied than of real dangers. Before the decisive moment arrives they have exhausted all the terrors of death and are prepared for the worst. The cold phlegmatic northern, on the contrary, goes with greater coolness into battle, but often finds it worse than he expected.

★★★★★★

I have suffered a severe loss; the only friend I had found here died a few days ago. Similar tastes and a like fate had drawn us together. He was of a good family at Berlin, as the high cultivation of his mind sufficiently proved; but an unfortunate longing for excitement and adventure had driven him from home. I am convinced that he died of

34

homesickness. He had never served before, and could not, therefore, brook this brutal and savage life so well as I could, and a fever hastened his death. He had written to his father for money to obtain his discharge, under the conviction that he could not endure his life here, and was in the daily expectation of an answer. His imagination already transported him back to his family; but he grew weaker every day and at length had to be carried to the hospital, where I visited him daily when my turn of service did not prevent me.

When I went yesterday and inquired after him, one of the attendants pointed to his bed: on approaching it I found him dead. No one, not even his next neighbour, had heard him die. He was buried next morning with no kind of ceremony, and I followed him to the grave alone. It is well for him that he is at peace! His spirit was too gentle to bear the sight of all this cruelty and wretchedness. One must case one's heart in triple brass to bear existence here at all.

Since the 1st of December our company has been quartered in Fort Duquesne, which stands upon the sea and defends the south-eastern side of the town. This fort is built upon a rock rising so abruptly from the sea that a few half-bastions towards the land are sufficient for its defence. A wooden shed has been erected to shelter the garrison from the weather.

We are uncommonly well off here, for the duty is not severe: most of our time is spent in fishing. The coasts of Africa abound with various sorts of fish which, to us at least, appear excellent; but indeed many circumstances combine to make us think so. A small kind of oyster, which is also met with in Spain, and sea-hedgehogs are particularly abundant. We only have to take them off the rocks, to open and eat them.

The starfish too are common here, and I have a strange tale to tell of one. During the month of August the soldiers were in the habit of bathing in the sea every evening, and from time to time several of them disappeared, no one knew how. Bathing was in consequence strictly forbidden, in spite of which several men went into the water one evening; suddenly one of them screamed for help, and when several others rushed to his assistance they found that a huge starfish had seized him by the leg with four of its limbs, whilst it clung to the rock by the fifth. The soldiers brought the monster home with them, and out of revenge they broiled it alive and ate it. This adventure sufficiently accounted for the disappearance of the other soldiers.

The rainy season, which generally lasts three or four months, has already set in accompanied by hurricanes of extraordinary violence, which fortunately last but a short time, though indeed quite long enough to cause the death and ruin of countless sailors. A few days ago a vessel was dashed to pieces against the very rock upon which the fort stands. It turned out to be a French merchant brig, which had anchored in the roads to avoid the raging of the elements.

Another night, while I was on watch, the storm increased by degrees to a perfect hurricane; the rain came down in torrents, and the darkness was such that it was impossible to see a yard before one's face. In a moment the wooden shed was unroofed, and the waves dashed over the very top of the rock. Next morning the fragments of a vessel lay at our feet; the roaring of the wind and waves had entirely overpowered the crash of the shipwreck. Every soul on board had perished except a little dog which stood wet and trembling on a jutting cliff and was with difficulty induced to come to us: he appeared to be still expecting his master.

The Mediterranean has scarce any tide, but the north or south wind affects the ebb or flow on the African coast though only to the depth of a few feet. After a few days of calm its blue waters are so clear that the fish and seaweed, some hundred feet below, look as though one might touch them. There is a peculiar charm in thus looking down into the secrets of Neptune's kingdom. I often lie for hours on a jutting cliff, watching the crowd of fish sporting below, and the tortoises, those drones of the sea, lazily basking on the surface of the waves.

My mind involuntarily reverted to my childhood, and to my mother's story of the enchanted prince whom a beautiful mermaid imprisoned in her crystal palace deep under the sea. After a hundred years, which passed like a few months, the charm was broken and the prince returned upon the earth to ascend the throne of his forefathers. But, alas! all was changed—his race was extinct and there was none that knew him; he himself had long since forgotten the language of men. Then he longed to return to his crystal prison and cast himself headlong into the waves.

At times I can scarce refrain from following the example of the enchanted prince and going to lead a harmless peaceful life with the fish, far from the rapacious envious race of men. But even this were vain, for under the water too there is strife, and greediness, and ambition—everything, in short, save calumny.

February, 1841.

For nearly two months we have not once been disturbed by the Kabyles, and we should have enjoyed a state of the most tranquil peace and content had it not been for the fleas. These bloodthirsty monsters are indeed the most terrible enemies we have in Africa—nothing can protect us from their hostilities. I assure you that Kabyles and panthers, nay, even tight boots, or a bad conscience, are not to be compared to them. They are worst in the wooden barracks and the blockhouses. One must be worn out with fatigue in order to sleep there at all, and then one wakes covered from head to foot with specks of blood.

On the night of the 4th of February, contrary to their usual custom, the Kabyles paid us a very well-meant visit. We lay in our barracks, not dreaming of any danger, when we were awakened at eleven o'clock at night by repeated shots, and by some bullets which came through the deal boards of our barracks. In an instant we were dressed; each man snatched up his musket, and went out. The shots came from a rock to the westward of the town and only separated from it by a small arm of the sea. By some strange neglect no blockhouse had been built on this spot, which commanded the town. The Kabyles had stolen through the line of blockhouses in the dark, and from this rock they now fired into the town with their long rifles with some effect. The companies soon fell into rank.

Lieutenant-Colonel Picolou, a cool determined officer, made his appearance immediately, and placed all the sentinels of the town on a battery exactly opposite the rock, to answer the fire of the Kabyles and thus to make them believe that the whole garrison was there: in the meantime we marched out at the gate in perfect silence, reached the rock unobserved, and fell suddenly upon their rear. At the very moment when they saw us and raised their wild howl, we gave them a volley and charged them with the bayonet. As the Kabyles are totally unacquainted with the use of it, they could offer us no effectual resistance although they were double our number. Those who were not killed threw themselves into the sea, for, being mostly good swimmers, they chose rather to trust to the tender mercies of the waves than to ours. But even the very elements conspired against them. The sea was very rough, and the waves dashed the poor fellows to pieces against the rocks. But few escaped to tell the mournful tale to their kinsfolk. We remained on the rock till the following morning.

We had only taken three prisoners, for in the heat of the skirmish the soldiers cut down every one. Some, indeed, had even cut off the heads of the wounded with their own *yataghans*. The *Commandant Superieur* rewarded these heroes with five *franc* pieces, and stuck the heads over the city gates, where they remained until the stench became intolerable. Truly I almost begin to think that we have learned more of the barbarous manners of the Kabyles, than they of our humanity and civilisation.

In two days, a few old men belonging to the almost annihilated tribe came to implore peace and the permission to remove and bury their dead, which latter request was granted. They also wished to ransom the three prisoners, one of whom was the son of their chief, and offered forty oxen for them, but the *commandant* demanded eighty and the negotiators were forced to depart without them. Greatly to the annoyance of the *commandant* and the astonishment of us all, one fine day the prisoners had disappeared. They had been confined in a dry cistern close to the sea and had, with inconceivable difficulty, worked their way through to it in one night, let themselves down into the water by means of their long woollen girdles, and swum to the other side.

This was no slight matter, as the coast is tolerably distant and one of the prisoners had his thigh shattered by a bullet. They then escaped safely through all the outposts. For eight whole days the Kabyles kept coming to fetch the dead bodies of their relations. Their joyful songs contrasted sadly with their melancholy faces. They were entirely crushed by this last blow, which they looked upon as a chastisement from *Allah*, because they had transgressed his command to wage no war by night. Most of the corpses had to be fished up out of the sea.

I watched them one morning at this employment. The Kabyles stood round a body they had just found, and drew the mantle from off the head. Scarce had an old Kabyle seen the features of the corpse, than he turned away his face to hide his tears; perhaps it was his son. And the soldiers who stood by jeered him!

Truly war is wild work; especially a war to the knife, such as this. It is lucky for us that custom renders us indifferent to our own dangers and miseries, but then we often grow equally indifferent to the woes of others.

March, 1841.

We have just heard that we are to have a new governor; no other than General Bugeaud who made the treaty with Abd-el-Kader, at Tafna. He is a vigorous, enterprising man, and great things are expected from him.

An expedition into the interior against the Bedouins is talked of, in which we are to take part; and we have already received orders to embark in a steamer for Algiers in a few days. Well, I shall not be sorry to make acquaintance with those houseless, wandering sons of the desert.

CHAPTER 4

Algiers

Buterback, April, 1841.

We reached the bay of Algiers in the evening of the 29th of March. The voyage was favourable, but I cannot say that it was pleasant; six hundred of us were squeezed together on the deck of a steamer. I am perfectly convinced that a pickled herring has more space allotted to it in the barrel than a soldier on board a French steamboat. In the Mediterranean, troops are always conveyed on deck, in the steamers at least.

The air here is mild enough for this, even in winter; but during the often-continued rains, one sometimes cannot help sighing for one's own fireside.

The coast is uninteresting all the way from Dschigeli to Algiers. There is nothing to be seen but hills—some covered with brush-wood, and others quite bare. There are but few valleys or streams, and scarce any human dwellings.

Near Budschia you discover from the sea a beautiful and fruitful vale watered by the River Summam. This is occupied by some of the most powerful Kabyle tribes, which give a good deal of trouble to the French garrison at Budschia. The town stands on an eminence commanding the mouth of the river and great part of the valley, and is enclosed by a line of blockhouses. Budschia is one of the oldest towns in Africa, as is proved by a Roman fort in tolerable preservation, and the remains of walls. There is a small bay here which affords good anchorage for vessels and protection against the south and west winds.

A species of monkey, as large as a pointer, abounds in these mountains. While we lay at anchor in the roadstead for a few hours, we had ample opportunity of observing the conduct of several families of these apes on a neighbouring rock. Curiosity drew many of them very near to us, and we were vastly amused by their strange antics; but as soon as any on board made the motion of shooting they skipped away, evidently well aware of its meaning. In one moment the fond mothers flung: their sons across their backs, and disappearedl behind the rocks. It is very difficult to get at these monkeys, as they live in caves which no human foot can reach, and their whole system of defence is excellent; their service of sentinels is as regularly organised as that of the Kabyles.

At about five leagues from Algiers the Atlas mountains gradually recede and give place to the great plain of Metidja, which is watered by the Arrasch and the Messafren. This plain is divided from the mountain in a peculiarly abrupt manner; it has not the undulating surface of other valleys, but is as flat as a table from the foot of the Atlas to the base of the Sahel range. The Metidja, varying from three to five leagues in breadth, forms a semicircle of about fifteen leagues, and touches the sea twice, at *Maison Carrée*, and just below Cherchell. It would be one of the most fruitful districts in the world if it had but more water; but the rivers get low even in the month of June, and the earth is so parched by the rays of the sun that all vegetation withers, and only begins to revive in October with the autumn rains. Close to the foot of the mountain and near the river, where the soil is kept moist by artificial means, the earth yields two crops of corn and three of vegetables in the year.

We landed immediately and marched the same evening to Buterback, whence I now have the honour of writing to you. Buterback was formerly the castle of a Moorish *grandee*; it stands on the topmost ridge of the Sahel, not far from the camp of Kouba. We have a glorious view of the sea on one side, and of the Metidja and the lesser Atlas on the other. Nearly every evening we see, on the Atlas mountains, the watch-fires of the wandering Bedouins, with whom we hope soon to make a nearer acquaintance. We are already preparing for a grand expedition into the interior.

The new governor, Bugeaud, is determined, it is said, either to subjugate or destroy all the hostile tribes. The greatest excitement prevails. Fresh troops are landed every day. The Foreign Legion has been reorganised: the four battalions of infantry are increased to six, and divided into two regiments. Our battalion, the third of the first regiment, is commanded by Colonel Von Mollenbeck who has succeeded Colonel Von Hulsen. Our new colonel is a German who has been long in the French service. He is brave, but seventy years of age is too

41

old for expeditions in Africa. Our regiment has got new muskets with percussion locks instead of the old ones.

The governor came a few days ago to inspect us, and was very gracious. He appears to be about fifty, and has an air of great determination and coolness. He is of the middle size and strongly built; his face is much sunburnt, but pleasing; and he would be taken for younger than he is, did not his snow-white hair betray his age. Bugeaud is a man of restless activity, and keeps everyone on the alert by his continual presence. At three every morning he gives audience, to which all who have any complaint to make are admitted. Expeditions are to be made from several different quarters at once; one from Oran, another from Mostaganem. and a third from hence. The governor will probably lead the expedition from Oran himself, and ours will be commanded by General Baraguai d'Hilliers, whom the soldiers call the Stumped Arm, because he lost the use of his left arm by a shot.

It is said that we shall stay here some time longer, and a short rest will indeed be most welcome to us. When not on duty. I wander about in the neighbourhood, for within the range of the blockhouses one is tolerably safe. Every inch of soil is most carefully cultivated, chiefly by Spaniards and Arabs; there are also a few Germans who sell the produce of their labour, generally fruit and vegetables, for high prices at Algiers. The Germans, who are chiefly from Alsatia and Rhenish Bavaria, do very well, as they need only work one quarter the time they would do in their own country to secure an existence. Wherever there is water they can grow three crops of vegetables in the year, especially of potatoes which cost more here than figs and oranges.

The day before yesterday I paid my friend Hassan a visit at the Plane Tree Café, which is only a mile or two from Buterback. He was greatly rejoiced to see me again. We retired to his little garden behind the house, and, with a smile, he brought out a few bottles of *Malaga*, which we proceeded to pour down our throats whilst we sat on the ground after the Eastern fashion conversing most philosophically. I had to recount to him all my adventures at Dschigeli, which caused him to stroke his beard fiercely, whilst he muttered one *caramba* after another.

I have been several times to Algiers, which is about a league and a half from Buterback, to take a nearer view of the curiosities there

The upper, which is the old part of the town, bears a striking resemblance to the old Moorish cities of Andaluzia, such as Cordova and Eccija. The streets are very narrow, and the houses have but few windows looking into the streets, and those few are defended by close gratings. All the houses are built round a spacious court, which, in the dwellings of the rich, is paved with marble and adorned with a fountain. The only difference is, that the Spanish cities were evidently built during the most flourishing times of the Moors, as the style of the houses in Spain is far grander and more ornate than of those in Africa.

Algiers contains a population of about forty or fifty thousand souls, two-thirds of which are Jews and Arabs, and the rest Frenchmen, Spaniards, and Italians. The habits of the Jews differ but little from those of the Arabs, and one may still perceive that they are children of the same forefather. But the sons of Ishmael now seem disposed to consider themselves as the lawful descendants of Abraham, and to treat the Jews as bastards. The Jews are distinguishable from the Arabs by their gayer clothes, and the unveiled faces of their women. The Jewesses are far more beautiful than the Arab women, because they are not treated as mere domestic animals, and therefore have an air of greater refinement.

Their dress is simple but pleasing, usually a blue or brown garment confined under the breast with a girdle; their long black, hair is held together by a circlet of gold or silver, or by a ribbon; their arms and feet are bare. Their deep jet-black eyes are wonderfully beautiful, and though their intense brilliancy is somewhat softened by the long silken eyelashes, yet woe to him who looks too deeply into them.

I toiled through the narrow streets up to the Casabah, the former residence of the *Dey*, the road to which is so steep that steps had to be cut in it. As I did not know the shortest path, it was at least two hours before I reached the top.

The Casabah stands on a *plateau* commanding the whole town. Gloomy-looking battlemented walls surround the palace, and are so high, as entirely to conceal the building within them; one fine tall palm tree alone overtops the wall. The palace contains a beautiful marble court and some splendid rooms, in which two French battalions are now quartered.

The Casabah itself is commanded by a fort built by Charles V. on a height above the town. The French were fortunate enough to carry this fort by a *coup de main*, whereupon the Casabah and the town were forced to capitulate. The *Dey* was living there in the most perfect security; all his treasures were deposited in the palace, and he was convinced that the high walls of the city would defy all the endeavours of the French to take what had already baffled the English and the Dutch.

The English, under Lord Exmouth, had taken one of the forts upon the sea, which they evacuated after twenty-four hours' possession, upon a treaty with the *Dey*. It is still called *Fort Vinyt-quatre Heures*.

At the time of the French occupation, Algiers was strongly fortified; besides the thick ramparts, which in some places are double, the town was defended by several bastions and three forts, which were in a very good state of defence. More especially the batteries on the sea, which protect the harbour, were exceedingly strong, and the French have since made considerable additions to all the fortifications. The town itself, however, from its shape and position, must always remain exposed to a bombardment from the sea. The Turks cared but little for this contingency, partly because the town contained but few handsome houses, and partly because most of the inhabitants were Jews and Arabs. The *Dey* is said to have asked the English Consul, after its bombardment by Lord Exmouth, how much it had cost us; and on hearing it put at some millions (of *francs*?) he frankly replied, that he would willingly have done it himself for half the sum.

After satisfying my curiosity here, I went into the lower town, and on turning down a fresh street I was met by the sound of a *mandoline* and of singing, accompanied by peals of laughter, which issued from the second storey of one of the houses; the songs were Arab, the laughter might be Arab, French, or German, I knew not which, but at all events it was most hearty. Of course I walked in, ascended the stairs, and found myself in the midst of a mixed company of Arabs, Jews, Frenchmen, and Italians, all seated together on cushions against the walls of a spacious room.

On a sort of platform near the window sat two Arabs singing, with two Arab girls beside them accompanying their songs on the *mandoline*. They were at that moment singing a love song, the constant burthen of which was "Nanina"; the whole company was in the most joyous mood. Every man had one or more bottles of wine before him, and it seemed as if they had all drunk repeated bumpers. I was astonished at this wonderful advance in civilisation and good fellowship. On either side of me I saw Arabs filled with wine, and Arab women with unveiled faces, returning the wanton glances of Christians with still more wanton eyes. Truly this change does honour to the French.

I sat down by an Arab soldier of the French allied cavalry, whose burning cheek betrayed that he had transgressed the commandment of the Prophet. He immediately drank to me in the most familiar manner, saying, with a laugh, "*Scherap bueno, jaule.*" (The wine is good, comrade.)

"*Bueno,*" answered I; for it was generous Spanish wine, such as is chiefly drunk here. He then asked me in broken French, whether the women of Europe were equal to its wine? As in duty bound, I answered in the affirmative, and described to him the charms and the excellence of my countrywomen until my Arab friend seemed well inclined to visit Europe. But when I told him that *Allah* bestowed but one wife on us Europeans, he shook his head, saying, "*Macasch.*" (Nay, nay.)

By this time it was late, and as I had to be at Buterback before night I took my leave. The gate Babazoun was soon far behind me, and I hastened on towards my destination, for the sun was fast declining towards the sea; but the boisterous laughter, and the long-drawn burthen of "Na-ni-na" were ringing in my ears the whole way home

CHAPTER 5

March Through the Desert

Duera, May, 1841.

Our battalion has been eight days at Duera, a fortified camp on the southern declivity of the Sahel, and we expect every moment to start on some great expedition. But even here we do not want occupation; for nearly every day we have to escort a transport of provisions, intended for Blidah, from Delhi Ibrahim to Buffarik.

Buffarik is another fortified camp and small village, which stands on the River Arrasch in the middle of the plain of Metidja. The soil is very productive, but the air so unhealthy that the village has been depopulated more than once.

We also frequently have to reconnoitre the neighbourhood, and to clear it of the Hadjutes. These fellows live in the western part of the Sahel, and are notorious for their audacious robberies which they are so bold as to extend to within a few leagues of Algiers. A few days ago they gave us a strong instance of their daring. On the 1st of May, just as we were going to hear mass, in honour of the saint's-day of Louis Philippe, two of the native *gendarmes maures,* who are employed as guides, came galloping up at full speed, their horses' flanks bleeding with the spur, and made some communication to the commander of the camp. A general march was immediately sounded, and in the course of five minutes our battalion was on its way towards a, blockhouse to the left of Delhi Ibrahim.

There was no beaten track, and we had to force our way through brushwood as high as ourselves with, which the mountains are almost everywhere covered by no means an agreeable occupation. We had marched about two leagues and a half without stopping, at a pace more like a trot than a walk, when we reached a blockhouse occupied by a company of the first battalion of our regiment. Here we halted.

Lieutenant Colonel Picolou exchanged a few words with the officer in command at the blockhouse, and we started again immediately. After crossing a deep ravine about a mile beyond the blockhouse, the horsemen at the head of our advanced guard suddenly drew up and their horses snorted and refused to advance. On coming up with them, we saw the cause. About fifty dead bodies, all naked and headless, were scattered about. This massacre had evidently but just taken place, as the blood was still streaming from their necks.

Some thirty Hadjutes had lured the captain in command of the blockhouse, a Swiss of the name of Müller, to leave it in pursuit of them, at the head of fifty of the garrison. At his approach the Hadjutes retreated across the ravine, and he was imprudent enough to follow them to a spot where he could receive no assistance from the blockhouse. He had scarcely reached the other side of the ravine when he was surrounded by above six hundred well-mounted Hadjutes. Captain Müller and his handful of men defended themselves to the last; many of them were separated and cut down singly; but their leader and about half of his people instantly formed into a square, and resolved to sell their lives as dearly as possible.

Their destruction was of course inevitable; and their bodies still lay as they fell, side by side, and there was not one among them that had not received several wounds. The number of dead and wounded horses scattered around showed how bravely they had fought. The Hadjutes had, as usual, carried away their fallen comrades. Of the fifty soldiers who had left the blockhouse one only escaped who, having been wounded at the beginning of the fight, had fallen among some thick brushwood, where he had lain concealed until the departure of the Hadjutes. He had thus been a spectator of the whole of this horrid scene, and had been forced to look on whilst the Hadjutes massacred his comrades and finally cut off their heads, which they bore away as trophies hanging to their saddle bows.

It cannot be denied that Captain Müller caused the destruction of his company by his rashness, but he paid for his fault with his life. Peace be to his ashes, for he met his death like a man. This scene of blood made a deep impression on me, as on all my comrades, whose countenances were some burning with rage and thirst for revenge, and others pale with terror and disgust. The corpses were immediately buried on the spot, the blockhouse garrisoned by a fresh company, and we marched back again.

During the whole way home I did not hear a single song nor one coarse jest, of which there were generally no lack; even the roughest and most hardened characters were shaken by that which they had just seen.[1] Everyone reflected that the fate of their comrades might one day be their own.

The blockhouse is about three leagues from Algiers, and one from Delhi Ibrahim; so you may judge tolerably well of what is meant by the French territory.

Blidah, June.

On the sixth of May we left Duera for Blidah, the rendezvous appointed for the troops which were to form the *colonne expeditionnaire.* For several days troops of every description, and an infinite number of mules laden with provisions had been passing through Duera.

Alter a march of two hours we left the Sahel mountains and descended into the plains of Metidja, where we proceeded, much at our ease, along a broad road which had been made as far as Blidah for the traffic of waggons. The lesser Atlas appeared to lie so close before us that we expected to arrive in a few hours at Blidah, the end of our day's march, which lies at the foot of that range. But the great height of the mountains deceived us, and it was noon before we readied Buffarik which is only half way; here we rested for two hours. Towards evening we at last saw Blidah just before us. A thick grove of orange trees had till then concealed it from our sight. The white cupolas of the numerous mosques, lighted up by the last rays of the setting sun, rose from among the bright green foliage of the oranges.

By the time we reached the town it was nearly dark, and we bivouacked under some old olive trees. I lay all night in a sort of waking dream and found it impossible to sleep. The soft air of the south, the intoxicating perfume of the orange flowers, the death-like stillness, rarely disturbed by the neighing of horses and the challenge of the sentinels—all this had such a magical effect on my senses, that I felt as though I was in the midst of one of the Arabian nights—it was not till

1. We are tempted to quote from *Two Years Before the Mast,* (by Richard Henry Dana. Jr. and is also published by Leonaur), a passage describing the effect produced by the sad spectacle of a man overboard:—"Death is at all times solemn, but never so much so as at sea; a man dies on shore, his body remains with his friends, and 'the mourners go about the streets;' but when a man falls overboard at sea and is lost, there is a suddenness in the event, and a difficulty in realizing it, which gives it an air of awful mystery. . . . . . All these things make such a death particularly solemn, and the effect of it remains upon the crew for some time. There is more kindness shown by the officers to the crew, and by the crew to one another. There is more quietness und seriousness. The oath and the loud laugh are gone."—Trans.

near morning that I fell asleep, and when I awoke the sun was already high in the heavens.

As we were to wait there a whole day for the arrival of the cavalry, I did not fail to take a nearer view of Blidah, which the Arabs justly call the Paradise of Africa. The town lies at the very foot of the Atlas, and for miles westward there extends a beautiful orange grove, the largest I ever saw, not even excepting that of Seville. Eastward, on the slope of the mountain, are fig and olive trees, interspersed with cedars which rival those of Mount Lebanon. Plentiful streams of water gush out of a ravine, and are conveyed in numerous channels through the streets of the town. The Arab sits beneath the arcade of his house, protected from the rays of the sun, bathing his feet in the cool spring water, and blesses *Allah* and the Prophet for his existence; and well he may, for his days glide tranquilly on, like the brook at his feet. Doubts and inward struggles are unknown to him; the Arab has but one God, one sword, and one horse, and wants nothing more.

In good and evil fortune he equally says, "The will of *Allah* be done," and bows his head to the dust. When I compared myself, a restless son of the north, to this Arab, truly, for the first time in my life, I was envious. But I soon reflected that it is impossible to retrace the path I have entered, and that, at the end of the dangers and difficulties which beset it, I too may rest beside a cool spring under a spreading tree.

In the plain, not very far to the west of Blidah, are the remains of a wall which evidently surrounded a town of considerable size. There is a tradition that it was destroyed by the Normans. I could never learn its name.

On the next morning at sunrise the whole column, consisting of about twelve thousand men, was in marching order, and the governor, who had arrived with the cavalry the day before, entrusted the command to General Baraguai d'Hilliers, and returned to Algiers from whence he was to proceed to Oran.

Our cavalry consisted, in several squadrons of the native *gendarmes maures*, besides a regiment and a half of French Chasseurs d'Afrique; the latter were all mounted on native horses, as European horses are quite worn out in the first half-year. The fourth regiment of *chasseurs*, who had just arrived from Bona, were mounted on Tunis horses which the *Dey* had sold to the French for a very moderate price; and nothing can be imagined more beautiful than this regiment. We had besides several field-pieces; for grenades and grape-shot do more execution among masses of cavalry than round-shot: each piece was served by four men and drawn by four mules. In the plain they were drawn by two mules, but in the mountain districts they were taken to pieces, and one mule carried the barrel, another the carriage, and the other two the ammunition. It requires only a few minutes to take the cannon to pieces and to put it together again.

We crossed the plain as far as the foot of the Col de Mussaia, which is about four leagues from Blidah, in three columns, surrounded by flying squadrons of French and native horse. The baggage, which was considerable, vas placed in the middle.

Besides what was loaded on mules, each soldier carried nine days' provisions, consisting of ship-biscuit, rice, coffee, and sugar. Bread and wine are not given on a campaign, owing to the very limited means of transport, for it would be impossible to use waggons, and the number of mules and donkeys required to carry the provisions for a march of five weeks is great enough as it is. Cattle are driven, and during an expedition each soldier is allowed double rations, that is, one pound of meat daily.

Besides his provisions, which are replaced from time to time, each soldier carries sixty rounds of ammunition, and a linen sack into which he creeps at night, and which stands him in stead of both an upper and under sheet. His only outer garment is the grey *capote*, which protects him against the summer's heat and the winter's rain; his stock of shirts is usually limited to the one on his back, which he washes in the first stream near his bivouac, and which is considered dry in ten minutes. The French set but little store by other articles of dress, but before they set out on a march they take care that each soldier be provided with a pair of good shoes; for shoes and arms are the first necessaries of the soldier on active service.

One may almost say, that to be well shod is even more essential than to be well armed; for the soldier can make no use of his weapons until he has reached the field of battle. The bravest troops are useless if they arrive too late, or leave one-third or half of their men lagging behind. It is impossible to lay too much stress upon the good marching order of the soldier. Marshal Saxe used to say, "*C'est dans les jambes qu'est tout le secret des manoeuvres et des combats: c'est aux jambes qu'il faut s'appliquer,*" and he was quite right.

The Dukes of Nemours and Aumale were with the column; the first as Brigadier-General, the latter as Lieutenant-Colonel of the Twenty-Fourth regiment of the line; both are tall and well made.

The Duke of Nemours generally wears the uniform of the Chasseurs d'Afrique, which suits him admirably, and follows the African fashion of wearing a thick beard round his mouth and chin; his younger brother has not yet followed this laudable example, most likely for the best of all reasons.

They are both much respected by the army as brave officers; and, indeed, they do their duty, on all occasions, even better than the other superior officers. The Duke of Nemours, however, in not so much beloved as the Duke of Orleans, as he is thought proud and aristocratic, whether justly or not I had no opportunity of telling.

The enemy did not attempt to molest us in the plain, although near the hills to our left we had constant glimpses of the white bernouses of the Bedouins, who, though too weak to make a regular attack, followed the column like jackals, and fell upon all that lagged too far in the rear.

For two years the Metidja has lain waste, but it is still covered with ruined dwellings and self-sown corn-fields, the traces of former cultivation.

With the exception of a few groups of olive trees, little wood is to be seen here; only the banks of a small stream called the Schiffa, are covered with laurels. We rested for some hours at the foot of the Col de Mussaia, before the column began to ascend the mountain.

This is the only pass in all this part of the lesser Atlas. The defiles in this narrow pass had been occupied by a few battalions of infantry the day before, as, without this precaution, the Bedouins might have crushed the whole army by merely throwing blocks of stone down the perpendicular rocks upon the troops defiling along the narrow path below.

The mountain scenery here is most wildly romantic: on the left are towering rocks, on the right a dizzy precipice; as far as the eye can reach there is nothing but tall brushwood, with a few olive trees and cedars wherever the soil is deep enough. No trace of human habitations was to be seen, the place appeared to be the abode of vultures and jackals, both of which abound. However, we afterwards learnt that the huts of the Kabyles are thickly scattered in all the defiles and glens, but they are so small and dingy as not to be visible from a distance.

From the foot of the Col de Mussaia up to its highest point is fully seven hours' march; and as the day was intensely hot, we shed many a drop of sweat.

Our battalion, which was the only one of the Foreign Legion engaged in this expedition, formed the rear guard, and we did not reach the top of the mountain until long after sunset.

The other troops had already encamped for the night, and we were sent on as outposts to the *Fontaine de la Croix*, a full league further, on the other declivity of the mountain. We went forward, limping and cursing. To make matters still worse, a guide was sent with us who did not know the way. At length, some tune past midnight, the sound of rushing waters announced to us that we had reached our destination. This *Fontaine de la Croix* derives its name from a huge cross cut into the living rock, probably by the Spaniards, as a pious memorial of their conquest. We had not much time for rest, as the signal for marching was given before sunrise. We were now the first of the advanced guard, and on we went, uphill and down dale. The Bedouins made an attempt to fire upon the column in a large olive grove, through which we had to pass at the foot of the Col, but our scouts and sharpshooters soon drove them off.

Medeah.

We reached Medeah, the end of our day's march, before noon. This city, one of the oldest in Africa, stands on a *plateau*, which terminates on two sides in an abrupt precipice, and is therefore easily defended. The town is surrounded by the most splendid fruit gardens; a Roman aqueduct still in good preservation, conveys water to it from a neighbouring mountain, and proves the high antiquity of the town. It is inhabited by Jews and Arabs, who seem devoted to the French—a disposition greatly encouraged by the presence of a French garrison of two battalions. Medeah was formerly the capital of the Beylick of Titteri, and the residence of the *Dey*.

We pitched our tents close to the town, beside a brook, where exquisite oranges, out of a garden close by, offered us some compensation for the fatigues we had undergone.

In spite of positive commands to the contrary, the soldiers proceeded to cut down the orange and almond trees for fuel, although there were plenty of large olive trees in the neighbourhood; but destruction is the proper element of the soldier.

Our bivouac usually forms a perfect square, modified of course by the ground; the infantry, who are outside, lie in double file behind their piled arms. Each battalion sends out one company as an advanced post, and another company remains within the lines as a picket. The baggage, artillery, and cavalry, are placed in the middle. The cavalry do not furnish any outposts, as horsemen, especially in broken ground, are too much exposed to the fire of the Bedouins and Kabyles, who steal singly towards us. The infantry, on the contrary, can more easily hide themselves, and by laying their faces close to the ground can hear the slightest sound. This is essential, as the Bedouins and Kabyles creep on all fours like wild beasts and fall upon single outposts, or shoot them from a distance when they can see them; for which reason the outposts change their ground after dark, to deceive the enemy. They generally draw back a little, leaving their watch-fires burning, which enables them to see whatever passes between them and the fire.

To our great satisfaction we stayed the whole of the next day at Medeah, as the general had directed many military stores and other matters to be forwarded thither. As it was Sunday, a solemn mass was celebrated on an eminence in the middle of the camp, by a priest who accompanied us, and who afterwards preached a very edifying sermon on peace. We were unfortunately so far from the priest that we heard nothing of the whole mass but an occasional solemn strain of military music.

We started next morning before sunrise, and continued our route due south. We marched several days without exchanging a single shot with the Bedouins. Our road lay always up or down hill; the heat was excessive and our marches were at the rate of from four to six leagues a-day.

In Africa it is, of course, impossible to say where or when the troops are to bivouac, as it depends upon finding wood and water. In case of need the wood can be dispensed with, as there is almost always enough to be found for cooking; but water is absolutely necessary for the cattle and the beasts of burden, which die if they get none after a long march; men can bear the want of it better. Of course, the general has several native guides who know the country, which is the more essential as the French have never been in this part of Africa before.

Had we not seen well-cultivated corn, barley, and rice fields in the valleys, we should have supposed that the whole of this district was uninhabited. As far as our cavalry scoured the country they found no traces of human beings save a few miserable little hovels made of rushes and skins of beasts, which we should have thought too wretched for a dog to live in. The owners, of course, were nowhere to be found. In former days this tract of country must have been thickly peopled, judging from the cemeteries which we saw from time to time. These were generally near the tomb of a *marabout*, and of enormous extent:

they might truly be called cities of the dead.

The graves were all exactly alike; no distinction seemed to exist among the dead. All were carefully covered with masonry, to keep the jackals from scratching up the bodies; and indeed no one can wonder that the Bedouins should wish to rest undisturbed in death after such restless wandering lives. Each grave was marked by a large upright stone, but no date told the dying day of him who lay beneath it, no *escutcheon* proclaimed his birth and descent.

The Bedouins, who are nomadic here as elsewhere, are too poor to buy tents, and accordingly they build for themselves in a few days the wretched hovels I have already mentioned. And the French make war upon these wretched houseless tribes! Truly, they might as well march against the jackals.

The Bedouins had placed *vedettes* on the tops of all the mountains to give notice of our approach. We could distinctly perceive on the distant hills, single horsemen in white *bernouses* who retreated as we drew near them.

We were now in the province of Titteri, among the mountains of the second Atlas range, which at this point is not divided by any considerable rivers or valleys from the lesser Atlas. It is impossible to tell where the one ceases and the other begins: all is mountain. Farther west, on the contrary, the extensive plain watered by the Schellif forms the natural division.

After several days' march the mountains which had hitherto been covered with mere brushwood became more wooded and romantic in their appearance. We passed through immense forests of olives, firs, and junipers, the latter of which grew to a considerable height. A great fire must have raged in one part of the forest, as nearly all the trees about it were black and charred. Some of them, however, still had so much vital power left that they had shot out afresh at top. Our column followed a caravan track through the wood.

It is remarkable that on the very highest point of all these mountains there stands a *marabout*. These *marabouts* are at the same time the temples and the mausoleums of the Bedouin priests, who are also called *marabouts*. They are usually small,—from thirty or forty feet square,— surmounted by a cupola, and commonly built of rough stone and whitewashed. Thus these houseless children of the desert, who have no abiding-place for themselves, yet build a house for their God.

One day our company was detached in order to cover the right flank; we were separated as sharp-shooters, and our road lay near one of these *marabouts*. The door was open, and curiosity impelled me and a few others to enter. We stepped in, and saw an old man in a white *bernouse* prostrate on the ground praying. It was indeed a spot well fitted for prayer and meditation; here, on the graves of his forefathers, so near to heaven, everything proclaimed the transitory nature of earthly things and the greatness and majesty of the Eternal.

As some of us approached him and made a noise, the priest arose and motioned us back with his hand, saying, "*No bueno Romis*" (not well Christians). We involuntarily drew back. The whole appearance of this man was that of an inspired prophet. We afterwards joked about it, but no one could conceive how this man came to be in a place so far from all human habitations. The Arabs and Bedouins call all Christians and Europeans by the name of *Romis*, *i.e.* Romans.

I do not know whether the jackals are particularly numerous in this district, or whether it is that they follow our column, but every evening after sunset they serenade us most melodiously. The jackal is not unlike our European fox, but it feeds chiefly on corpses and carrion, and is therefore dangerous only to the dead.

It is curious that the hoarse croaking bark of the hyena is always heard together with the howling of the jackal. The natives assert that every pack of jackals is led by a hyena. These serenades are not very enlivening. But though the howling of hyenas and jackals was my regular lullaby, and my knapsack my only pillow, I did not sleep a whit the less soundly after a good day's march.

By degrees the country grew more and more desert and treeless. The hills were bare and the valleys afforded but little water, and that little was fetid. The streams were already dried up; in the deepest places a little water was still standing, but it was so bitter that it could scarcely be used for cooking. It was only here and there that we found fresh springs. We suffered cruelly from heat and thirst: each man filled his flask every morning, but the water was soon drunk during a forced march, and it is not every one that knows how to make the most of it.

During the first part of the day as little as possible should be drunk, and even later a very small quantity, and that only while at rest; much drinking merely heats and weakens. When we halted at mid-day and found water we generally made some coffee, which even without sugar or milk was most refreshing. Before starting in the morning we usually drink coffee, in which we soak our biscuit. In the evening we make soup of the meat which is given out; so, you see, we cannot be accused of gluttony at any rate. But, indeed, this heat takes away all appetite, and one longs for nothing but a shady tree and a gushing fountain; all else is vain.

It is strange to see the efforts made by every creature when we are coming near a spring or a brook to reach it quickly. The weary faces of the soldiers resume their animation; the horses and mules who smell the water half a league off begin to neigh: and on reaching the water both men and beasts plunge into it, to satisfy their burning thirst. General orders and sentinels are of no avail; what is punishment or even death to the soldier at such a moment! He would much rather die by a bullet than by thirst. Most of them lose all self-control, and drink till they are literally full. I have seen some of them drink with a small tin can called a *quart*, which each soldier carries hanging to his button-hole, as much as five or six pints at a time. It is extraordinary that more do not die of it; but the water is generally warmed by the sun, and the subsequent marching brings on profuse perspiration.

Cailah.

Here, where one would least expect to find human beings, the Bedouins have begun to show themselves in great numbers, and to attack the flanks and the rear of the column, Perhaps they have been retreating before us all this time, and now that we draw near the lesser desert they are determined to retreat no further, by degrees their numbers increased, and without offering any resistance to the head of the column they hovered round us all day, greeting ns with wild yells of "*Lu, lu*" which probably meant "*Allah.*"

They gallop without any order, and singly, to within eighty or a hundred paces of our sharp shooters, and discharge their rifles at full speed. The horse then turns of his own accord, and the rider loads his piece as he retreats; and this is repeated again and again all day long.

The Bedouins never wait for a close encounter hand to hand when charged by our cavalry; they disperse in all directions, but instantly return. The only difference between them and the Numidians, of whom Sallust says. "They fight flying, and retreat, only to return more numerous than before," is, that the Numidians of old fought with bows and the Bedouins have rifles.

This kind of fighting is equally dangerous and fatiguing to us. It is no joke to be firing in all directions from sunrise till sunset, and to march at the same time, for we seldom halt to fight at our ease. The general only orders a halt when the rear-guard is so fiercely attacked as to require reinforcement. Any soldier of the rear-guard who is wounded or tired has the pleasant prospect of falling into the hands of the Bedouins and having his head cut off by them. One comfort is, that this operation is speedily performed: two or three strokes with the *yataghan* are a lasting cure for all pains and sorrows.

There are, it is true, a certain number of mules and litters to carry the sick and wounded; but on so long an expedition as this the number of the sick increases to such a degree that in the end every means of conveyance is overloaded. The only resource, then, is to unload the provision mules, and to distribute rations for eight or ten days more among the soldiers. In the end, however, both men and mules are dead beat, and every one must shift for himself. It requires long habit, and much suffering, before a man can bear to see his comrades butchered before his eyes without being able to help them.

For several successive days we were attacked with such pertinacity by the Bedouins, and their allies the Kaybles, that we supposed we must be coming upon their den, and so indeed it turned out. One evening, after a hot forced march, we saw on a mountain top, which formed a *plateau*, a great heap of stones which we knew to be a town. In two hours we were close upon it. Our battalion and several others climbed the steep hill, in order to enter the town from above, while the rest of the column attacked it from below. We were driving the Bedouins before us all the time.

At length we reached the walls, which were low and battlemented, but to our astonishment no one appeared to defend them, and the gates stood wide open. Suspecting a stratagem, some of us climbed to the top of the walls to look into the town. The nest was empty, and the birds flown; as usual we had come just too late. The whole column poured into the town, which was I think called Callah, and the soldiers eagerly ransacked the houses. The owners could not have been gone long, for the *kuskussu* on the hearth was still hot. A few fowls, cats, and lambs, which the Kabyles had left behind in their hurry, and two rusty cannons, were all the spoil. A far greater god-send was a fine spring of water near the city gates. Here we made up for the thirst we had endured all day.

After taking as much wood as was wanted to cook our supper, we set fire to the town. We then bivouacked on an eminence at a distance, where we slept as soundly as if we had performed some glorious action.

The soldiers began to grow impatient; we were now close to the lesser desert, without apparently being a bit the nearer to Abd-el-Kader's castle, which was the object of the expedition. They began as usual to invent the most extraordinary theories, some asserting that the general had sold us to Abd-el-Kader, others that we were in a few days to fight a battle against the Emperor of Morocco, although we were then further from Morocco than from Algiers.

The Lesser Desert.

One morning before leaving our bivouac, we were ordered to fill our kettles with water, and to carry some wood upon our knapsacks, as we should have to pass the night in the desert. After two hours' march the desert lay before us, and a most cheerless prospect did it afford. To the south nothing was to be seen but an undulating surface of shifting sand: on the east and west alone, the Atlas range was still visible.

The palm grows better than any other tree in this scorching soil; but it was only from time to time that we found one, and then so stunted and withered was it that it could afford no shelter to the weary wanderer. The palm is seldom found in groups, generally single, or at most in twos and threes, for which reason the natives call the palm tree the hermit.

We had of course no idea how far the desert might extend, and felt as desolate and fearful as the young sailor who for the first time sees his native shore fade from his sight. To our great joy we soon turned westward, always following the track of a caravan. The march was excessively fatiguing, as no breath of air tempered the burning heat under which we toiled along, up to the ankles in sand. I was so tired, that I could have exclaimed with King Richard, "*A horse! a horse! my kingdom for a horse.*"

Towards evening we reached a spot which the Bedouins had but lately quitted, as we saw by the traces of tents and herds. To our great joy we found several deep cisterns containing some water, not indeed fit to drink, but good enough for cattle and for cooking. These cisterns are filled during the rainy season, and some water remains in them till far into the summer. Next day we turned still more to the west, and towards evening we reached the foot of the mountains, where we bivouacked beside a brook, whose waters had called forth luxuriant vegetation. We were not a little rejoiced to escape from the accursed desert. Many of us had already bidden *adieu* to life, and fancied that we saw our bones lie bleaching on the burning sand.

The green banks of this small stream where we lay seemed to us a perfect paradise. On the following morning we followed the course of the brook upwards with more than usual speed, preceded at some distance by the cavalry, whence we supposed something must be in store for us. Towards mid-day some Bedouins showed themselves one by one on our right flank, and discharged their rifles at the column. As the whole body of cavalry had been sent forward, sharp-shooters were detached, who succeeded in keeping the Bedouins at a respectful distance. By degrees, however, they came in greater numbers, and grew bolder, so that our sharpshooters had to be constantly reinforced and relieved. It is most fortunate for us that the Bedouins have such a holy horror of the bayonet. The sharp-shooter may feel perfectly secure against an attack hand to hand with the *yataghan* from any single Bedouin.

They confine themselves to swearing and shooting at him, both always at full gallop; and as the aim of a horseman is far less certain than that of a foot soldier, the sharp-shooter has the advantage. The Bedouins fight hand to hand only when they are greatly superior in numbers, or when a small band is cut off from the main body; then, indeed, the danger is very great.

Thaza.

Towards evening we at length saw on a height before us the castle of Abd-el-Kader. The object of our expedition. It was a large square building in the European style, surrounded with high walls.

Close to it blazed a village which the Bedouins had fired with their own hands. The cavalry had taken the castle without a single blow, for the Arabs had just deserted it.

Every soul had fled, leaving nothing but bare walls. We had again arrived too late, and I thought of the words of my friend Hassan, "Quickness is the soul of war." I am convinced that we are very deficient in cavalry, more especially in native horsemen, who know every hole and corner in the defiles, and whose horses can scramble anywhere. Our cavalry is not nearly strong enough to act for several days independently of infantry and artillery. Possibly, too, the general was not particularly well served by his spies and guides, or some one of those thousand accidents may have occurred which cause the failure of even the best laid plans.

We bivouacked immediately under the castle walls, for it was late, and both men and horses were too tired to pursue the enemy. We all rushed into the castle to see the inside, and, if possible, to plunder; but nothing was left except a good many sheepskins and a few carpets.

The whole construction of the castle plainly showed that it had been built under the direction of European architects. The rooms of the *emir* alone were arranged in the Arabian manner. The European prisoners had been confined in the vaults below, where we found the names of people of all nations written on the walls. Some bewailed that we should come too late, and that they were to be transferred to some other dungeon, they knew not w here. Many prisoners of condition had been shut up there; among others, a French *Sous Intendant*, who had been seized by a horde of Bedouins near Duera, not far from Algiers. This man was afterwards sent back without ransom, upon the intercession of the Bishop of Algiers, who wrote to Abd-el-Kader about him.

It is but just to add, that the prisoners of Abd-el-Kader, who were subsequently released, said that he had treated them very humanely. It is true that they worked at his buildings, but they had enough to eat, and were not beaten. As soon however as the *emir* was gone on a distant expedition, they were shamefully ill-used, and after a hard day's work got only a handful of barley and a little oil,—a poor repast for those accustomed to the strong meat of the north. I have since met with a Dutchman who had passed three years in this slavery, at the end of which he was exchanged: hunger and misery had rendered him completely imbecile. He had lost all sense of taste and smell, and swallowed indiscriminately everything that was placed before him, whether good or bad.

We stayed here the following day to rest. The cavalry went out to reconnoitre whether any of the Bedouins still lay hidden in the defiles and valleys, but returned without having found any traces of them. These people have a peculiar art of driving away large herds of cattle with incredible rapidity. The engineers completely destroyed the castle by blowing up the walls, and setting all the wood that was in it on fire.

To the great joy of us all, a march back to Milianah was ordered. But before reaching the plains of the Schellif we had to cross the arm of the Uanseris mountains, at the cost of infinite suffering and fatigue.

On the second day we came to a defile, at least five leagues in length, and so narrow that in many places we had to march in single file. On either hand rose lofty and precipitous rocks, which the infantry were forced to occupy and defend.

Before daybreak these positions were taken without much difficulty, for the Bedouins had already deserted them. The infantry and cavalry, posted on the heights on either .side of the pass, covered the advance of the column, and the main body and the artillery began to defile through; this took so much time that the head of the column had already debouched before the rear had begun to move. It is scarcely conceivable how, with the column drawn out over at least five leagues of ground, we escaped without a mishap.

Considerable masses of cavalry showed themselves on our right flank, and made several attacks on us, but all so feeble and unconnected that they were easily repulsed. We bivouacked upon a *plateau* on the side of the defile, but the rear-guard did not reach the spot until late in the evening. In a few days more we reached the Schellif, which the natives call the great river,—a name it by no means deserves at this place, where it is small and insignificant; but the youthful impetuosity with which it dashes over rocks and hollows gives promise of its future size. We followed its course for several days, marching sometimes on the right, sometimes on the left bank, on account of the narrowness of the valley; and having no pontoons with us, we had the pleasure of wading through the stream several times a day.

The rivers in Africa are seldom so deep as not to be fordable; but the health of the soldiers is destroyed by constantly marching in wet clothes, more especially in the morning and evening when they do not soon dry. I am convinced that many illnesses, particularly fevers and diarrhoea, are brought on by this. Besides, the soldiers' feet suffer terribly from the softening of the skin and the hardening of the shoes.

By dint of scouring the country in all directions, our cavalry at last succeeded in surprising a tribe and taking two or three prisoners and a few hundred sheep, which barely supplied us with meat for one day. It was fortunate that we had such a quantity of livestock with us, for we must otherwise have died of hunger. As it was, our poor oxen were grown so thin, owing to forced marches and want of food, that Pharaoh's lean kine would have seemed fat in comparison.

By-and-by we reached the end of the Uanseris mountains, where the valley of the Schellif widens into an extensive plain which we found covered with corn, although no tents or huts were to be seen. As the wheat and barley were still too green to burn, the column deployed to its utmost breadth, so as at all events to trample down the crops as much as possible.

Milianah.

The further side of the plain is skirted by the lesser Atlas range, on the southern declivity of which stands Milianah, whose white walls and mosques we distinctly saw from afar.

Towards evenings we reached the foot of these mountains, and bivouacked immediately under Milianah. On the following day, whatever ammunition and provisions we had remaining, about, eight days' supply, were sent into the town. Immediately above Milianah is the highest point of the lesser Atlas, and the town is built half way up the mountain, on a *plateau*, which falls abruptly on three sides. This was formerly the residence of Abd-el-Kader, who showed great judgement in the choice of a spot so easily defensible and commanding the fruitful plain of the Schellif. A beautiful clear stream which gushes out of a hollow above the town, runs through the streets, and serves to work the powder mills and manufactories established by Abd-el-Kader.

In 1840, when the war broke out between Abd-el-Kader and the French, Milianah was besieged and taken by the latter. One half of the besiegers assailed the town from below, while the rest having succeeded in planting some cannon on a height commanding the town, poured their shot down upon it. When Abd-el-Kader saw that he could hold the place no longer, he determined to retreat by the only gate which was still free, and first rode sword in hand through the streets, cutting down every one that would not follow him. Nearly all effected their retreat in safety, and most of the families settled on the northern slope of the lesser Atlas. The town contains few buildings worth looking at, except the palace of the *emir*. The French have repaired and considerably strengthened the fortifications of the place.

With Milianah Abd-el-Kader lost the valley of the Schellif, and was compelled to retire as far as the Mina. He transported his wives and children and his most valued property to Tekedempta, a rocky fastness in the greater Atlas, beyond Mascara.

From Milianah the column marched towards the Col de Mussaia, which we had to pass again. Next morning, when we were still about twenty leagues from this accursed Col, General Changarnier was sent in advance with four battalions of infantry, of which ours was one, some cavalry, and a few fieldpieces to occupy the positions in the pass Those who were not in good walking order were left behind with the column. We started at four in the morning, and marched the whole day, only halting for ten minutes at a time, till we reached the *Plateau des Reguliers*, (so called from Abd-el-Kader's regular troops, who often encamp there,) which lies at the foot of the Col. Evening had already begun to close in.

The day had been excessively hot, and the forced march had fatigued us so much, that it was absolutely necessary to halt and to give the soldiers time to cook their soup and to recover a little. In two hours we were to start afresh. The soldiers were indignant at such an unusually long and rapid march, and railed at the harshness and cruelty of the general, who they said sacrificed his men to a mere caprice.

The soldiers, of course, could not see the need for such excessive haste; some poor fellows moreover had been left on the road for want of mules to carry them. I several times heard the exclamation, "I wish that the Bedouins would grow out of the ground by millions and put an end to us all." The fatigues and hardships of this kind of war at last produce perfect indifference to life, which becomes a mere burden. Indeed it is an old saying, *"That nothing is better calculated to render the soldier careless of danger than fatigue and privation."*

When Sylla was made commander of the Roman forces against Mithridates, he found the Roman legions so enervated by ease and luxury that they were afraid to face the enemy; but Sylla worked them and marched them about till they besought him to lead them to battle. He then attacked the enemy and beat them.

General Changarnier, who commanded us, is known by the whole army as a brave soldier who exacts the very utmost from others as well as from himself, and who accordingly most often succeeds in his enterprises. He is more feared than loved by the men; who say, "*C'est un homme dur ce Changarnier.*" He appears to be a few years above fifty, powerfully built, but with a head somewhat weather-beaten by the storms of life. He has been fighting in Africa ever since the first occupation.

After two hours' rest, when night had completely closed in, we started again in perfect silence, and left our watch-fires burning to make the enemy believe that we were going to bivouac on the *plateau*; we wound up the mountain, which is far steeper on this side than even on the other. This night was one of the most painful of my whole life. The oppressive heat and forced march had so exhausted us that we marched more asleep than awake, and were only roused by striking our feet against a stone, or our noses against the knapsack of the man before us. From time to time we were reminded of our danger by the order "*Serrez! Serrez!*" and indeed it was necessary to keep close, for whoever lagged behind was lost.

We all dropped down asleep during the short stoppages which inevitably took place at the difficult passages; and without doubt we left behind us many sleepers, who were not perceived by the rear-guard and instantly fell a prey to the Bedouins. About four o'clock in the morning we passed the *Fontaine de la Croix*, where we bivouacked on our former march; thus we still had a league to march before reaching the highest point of the Col. From this spot the battalions separated, in order to ascend the various heights. By five we were at the top, almost without firing a shot.

These positions are so impregnable that the Bedouins could have driven us back merely with stones if they had had any resolution. I am convinced that the Kabyles of Budschia and Dschigeli would have sent us home in a fine plight. As we had to wait for the arrival of the main body, we established ourselves on the mountain top as well as we could. Greatly to our annoyance, however, no water was to be found in the neighbourhood, and we were obliged to fetch it a whole league from the *Fontaine de la Croix*.

Towards mid-day, when the fog cleared off, we discovered the blue Mediterranean beyond the plain of Metidja and the Sahel mountains. We greeted it as our second home, with loud cheers and cries of "Land," for the sea was to us what the harbour is to the sailor after a long and perilous voyage. From this point, one of the highest of the lesser Atlas, we enjoyed the most glorious prospect. On one side we saw the vast plain of Metidja and the sea beyond it; on the other, several small valleys, where pastures still green proved the fruitfulness of the soil. In one of these little valleys we espied a few huts and a flock of sheep grazing in peaceful ignorance of their danger. This time the poor inhabitants of the hovels were protected by their poverty: had the prey been better worth taking, a division of cavalry would soon have been down upon them.

The sharp and broken outlines of the mountains and the dark foliage of the olives, pines, and cedars, which clothe their sides, give a singularly wild and sombre character to the Atlas range. The air at this height is sharp and piercing even in summer; and while we could scarcely breathe for the heat below, we here buttoned our capotes up to our very chins. This appeared to be the land of vultures and eagles, which soared and screamed around us by hundreds, apparently highly offended at their unexpected guests. They came so near to us that several of them were shot by the soldiers with split bullets; but they were a perverse and stiff-necked generation, which even when mortally wounded did not cease from biting and clawing.

The main body arrived towards evening, and on the following morning we continued our march towards the Metidja, with great alacrity and good humour. Our knapsacks were light, and the prospect of making up at Blidah for the hardships we had undergone infused new life into all of us.

At noon we were already at the foot of the mountains, and a few hours later the mosques and orange groves of Blidah lay before us.

It was indeed high time for us to return to the camp, for the number of sick had increased frightfully of late; horses, mules, and donkeys were all overloaded with them, and many a one who would long since have been given over by the physicians in Europe still crawled in our ranks. Our shoes and clothes were in rags; many even had wound pieces of ox hide about their feet in default of shoes. We bivouacked close by the town on the bank of a small brook.

All the people in the town came out to see us and to convince themselves that we were still alive, for it had been reported several times that the column was utterly destroyed. They lifted up their hands in amazement at our deplorable appearance; and it was only on comparing ourselves with these sleek and well-fed citizens that we perceived how wild and wretched we looked, and that our faces were dingy yellow, and our bodies dried up like so many mummies. I am convinced, that except on the persons of the attendants on the sick, and some of the superior officers, not even Shylock himself could have cut one pound of flesh out of the whole column.

Arabs, Jews, and Christians vied with each other in offering us wine, fruit, bread, &c., at very sufficient prices, for in Africa nothing is *gratis*.

All discipline was now at an end: the officers were soon dispersed among the various *cafés* and *restaurants*, and the soldiers bought as much bread, fruit, and wine as they could get for their few *sous*, and seated themselves under the first shady tree they could find, where they drank till all the miseries of life were forgotten.

CHAPTER 6

The Prisoners

After stopping eight days to repair the state of our arms and shoes, the column marched again to provision Milianah. and to lay waste the plains of the Schellif with fire and sword. All the cavalry, save two squadrons, were dismounted, and their horses loaded with all sorts of provisions, rice, meal, coffee, sugar, &c. As we left Blidah rather late, we were forced to pass the night on this side of the Col de Mussaia, in an olive grove at the foot of the mountain. In all my life I never saw so many small birds as in this grove; it was positively alive with them. They twittered and warbled in all tongues; the bullfinches especially delighted me with a melody so like that which they sing in my own country, that I fancied I recognised some old acquaintances among them. The soldiers contrived to catch a number of young birds, who, dreaming of no danger had ventured out of their nests, and to cook them for supper.

On the following day we ascended the Col; not indeed without fatigue, but with infinitely less than the first time, for we were already steeled by habit. We bivouacked on the *Plateau des Reguliers*, at the opposite foot of the mountain.

We reached the plains of the Schellif in two days without molestation. The heat began to be intolerable to us in this region, bare of trees, and surrounded by high mountains, which shut out every breath of air. Towards mid-day we could scarcely breathe, and many of our number perished from thirst and fatigue, some died on the spot; they suddenly fell down backwards, foaming at the mouth, and clenching their hands convulsively, and in ten minutes they were dead. To add to our distresses, a body of three or four thousand Arab horsemen appeared on our left flank, headed by Abd-el-Kader in person.

We were in the most awkward position in the world; all our cavalry, save two squadrons, was dismounted, and the column scattered over a space of at least two leagues. I am convinced that if Abd-el-Kader had made a determined attack upon us at that moment he might have annihilated the whole column. Instead of this, only a few irregular parties of horsemen galloped towards us, discharged their rifles, and retreated. Once or twice a considerable number of Arabs assembled together, as if preparing to attack us. But our general immediately ordered some grenades to be thrown among them out of a few fieldpieces, and the whole body was scattered like chaff before the wind.

This want of resolution in our enemies was extraordinary, for Abd-el-Kader must have known our position, and even if he had not a single spy, he could perceive it with his own eyes. We saw him several times within musket-shot, galloping about with his attendants, to give orders. I believe that this inaction was owing to no want of courage or capacity in him, but to the character of the Bedouins, and to their peculiar mode of warfare, which nothing can induce them to alter. They never attack *en masse*, except when they can overwhelm the enemy with their numbers. By this practice the Bedouins have drawn upon themselves the reproach of cowardice from the French: whether with justice is not for me to decide; but I think that much might be said on behalf of the Bedouins.

It is quite true that they have no courage collectively. The reason is, that they want those ties by which masses are held together,—a higher degree of civilisation, and a leading idea,—either love of a common country, or religious enthusiasm. The former is unknown to the Bedouin, whose tribe is his country, and whose next neighbour is often his bitterest foe: he is never, like the Arab, deeply imbued with religion; to him *Allah* is a mere god of plundering and murder. To these causes is added the custom of a thousand years; these tribes have known no other mode of warfare since the days of the Numidians.

The Bedouin conception of bravery and of cowardice is totally unlike ours. He sees no cowardice in retreating before a superior force, and returning to the charge at a more favourable opportunity, but necessary prudence—a quality which stands as high in his estimation as valour. The Bedouin would never shrink from the European in single combat, and frequently surpasses him in endurance of privations, and even of death, which he meets with the resignation of a philosopher.

We afterwards heard that Abd-el-Kader had endeavoured by every means in his power to induce the chiefs to make a regular and organised attack upon the column, but all in vain. That very evening we reached the foot of the mountains just below Milianah, and the favourable moment for attacking us was past,

Abd-el-Kader is a handsome man of about thirty-seven or thirty-eight. Although dressed in the common Bedouin *bernouse* and turban, he was easily distinguishable from his attendants by the splendour of his arms and of his horses. Even from a distance I thought I could trace on his dark and bearded countenance the intrepidity and religious enthusiasm by which he is distinguished, his bearing was proud and noble. I could not help watching this man with a certain degree of admiration, for he alone is the soul of the whole resistance to the French; without him no three tribes would act in common. I heartily wished him a better fate; for his lot will be either to fall in battle, or to be betrayed by his friends, like Jugurtha, to whom he may well be compared, although to equal courage and perseverance he unites an elevation of character not ascribed to the Numidian of old by historians, who indeed were nowise impartial.

Abd-el-Kader has strictly forbidden his soldiers to kill the prisoners in cold blood, and in order to put a stop to this practice among the Bedouins, he pays ten Spanish dollars for every living captive. The *emir* received an almost European education from his father, who was a *marabout* highly venerated by the people, and who lived for several years in Italy, where he became acquainted with European habits and manners.

Abd-el-Kader exercises great influence over both the Bedouins and the Arabs, from being their ecclesiastical as well as temporal ruler: he is the *Khaleefeh* (Vicegerent of the Prophet), I have seen one of the Arabs of our own allied cavalry reverentially touch the earth with his brow on hearing the name of Abd-el-Kader; but his veneration would nowise have deterred him from murdering or taking prisoner the *Khaleefeh* and his whole *zemala*.

The column bivouacked at the foot of the mountain, where we had one whole day's rest, while the provisions and ammunition intended for Milianah were being carried up into the town. It was the turn of our company to furnish outposts,—a service which recurred every sixth day, and I was sent with twelve others to the outermost line.

At the foot of these mountains there is an abundance of water such as is rarely seen in Asia. Streams gushed out of the ravines and covered the surrounding country with the most luxuriant vegetation. There was an equal abundance of snakes, which we could well have spared. We had established ourselves behind a clump of wild olives to protect ourselves from the scorching rays of the sun, and I had formed a sort of small arbour and lain down under it to sleep, so as to be fresh for the night, when of course rest was out of the question.

Scarce had I fallen asleep when I was roughly shaken and called by my name. I jumped up and seized my arms, thinking that at the very least Abd-el-Kader and his whole army were upon us, when my comrades showed me a huge snake coiled up behind my knapsack. It gazed enquiringly at us with its wise-looking eyes, and glided away into the bushes as soon as we attempted to seize it. We now held a council of war; for although the snake had as yet behaved with great propriety, we thought the presence of such guests during the night highly unwelcome. We accordingly resolved to set fire to the brushwood, and before long it was in a blaze.

Presently our friend slipped out in haste and tried to take refuge in some bushes close by; but we fell upon it with sabres and muskets, and one of us at last succeeded in pinning it to the earth with his bayonet just behind the head. The creature hissed and lashed fiercely with its tail, but all in vain, its last hour was come. Its head was severed with a sabre from its body, which continued to move for several hours. When we left the spot in the morning the chief *matador* hung the snake round his neck as a trophy, and it was so long as nearly to touch the ground on both sides, so that it measured eight or nine feet at least.

We had not marched far over some marshy ground covered with rushes and withered grass, when the battalions just before us separated as if by word of command, and another snake darted in long curves down the middle. We instantly made way for it to pass. The snake seemed in a great hurry and instantly disappeared among the rushes. One of the chief discomforts of Africa is the number of creeping things, poisonous as well as harmless, and of wild beasts. They are all, however, far less dangerous to man than is generally supposed.

At any rate bodies of men have nothing to fear from them, as they invariably retreat before an advancing column. They only attack human beings when urged by the utmost necessity, either of self-defence or of hunger. I can only remember two instances of solitary sentinels being attacked and torn in pieces in the night by hyenas, which are indeed the most dangerous of all animals, as they kill for the mere pleasure of killing, and not from hunger. There is also a great plenty of lizards, scorpions, tarantulas, and all such vermin.

The scorpions generally lurk under the small stones; and great care should always be taken in lying down to sleep, not to move them and thus disturb the scorpions, which might then crawl over one's hands or face and sting them. Land tortoises abound in the marshy spots where the soldiers hunt for them during the march and eat them for supper. They afford an excellent soup and their flesh is as tender as chicken.

We marched only about two leagues and then bivouacked on the further bank of the Schellif, in the very middle of a fine wheat field. The whole left bank, as far as the foot of the mountains, was covered with wheat and barley just ripe for the sickle.

We saw nothing more of Abd-el-Kader, who had marched westward along the left bank of the Schellif the day before with all his cavalry. From our bivouac we could trace his route by the clouds of dust. He, probably, perceived that he had missed the favourable opportunity of attacking us.

The column remained three days on the same spot, diligently employed in cutting as much corn as possible, and in conveying it to Milianah on every available horse, mule, and donkey in the camp. The harvest was so abundant as to supply the town for a whole year. On the fourth day we followed the course of the Schellif, burning the standing corn as we went. We did not, like Samson, set fire to the corn fields of the Philistines by driving into them three hundred foxes, with burning torches tied to their tails. We had the advantage of the experience of ages, and the noble inventions of modern times over the Israelite hero.

Lucifer matches were distributed among the rear-guard, with which the crops were fired. We were once very near suffering from this proceeding. Some roving Arabs had thoughtlessly set fire to the corn on one side of the column: the wind blew from that quarter, and in a moment the whole column was enveloped in flames. Fearful disorder ensued, the terrified beasts of burden ran in all directions, and the smoke was so thick as to prevent our seeing the troops before us. A resolute enemy might at that moment have cut the whole column to pieces.

After a march of two days we crossed back again to the right bank of the Schellif, over the only bridge we ever found in the interior of Africa. It had five arches, and appeared to be Roman, was built of hewn stone, and as perfect as if only finished yesterday. At the distance of one day's march beyond this bridge the valley of the Schellif becomes exceedingly narrow; the river pent between high mountains, rushes like a torrent: ten or twelve leagues further the valley again widens into a plain.

We bivouacked upon a *plateau* on the right bank of the river. The heights around us were covered with wild olives and dwarf oaks, and the valleys with the finest ripe corn. As the general had reason to suspect that we were near some rich Kabyle tribes, we remained on this spot for several days, during which the cavalry and some chosen bodies of infantry made excursions into the surrounding country every morning before dawn, and returned triumphant and loaded with booty every day.

During all this time the number of sick increased fearfully: the forced marches, the excessive heat, and the quantity of meat which the soldiers ate without any other food but bad sea-biscuit, undermined their health. Diarrhoea and fever prevailed in every division. The mules were soon so loaded that many who could no longer drag themselves along were rejected and left to die on the road.

The troops were so thoroughly disheartened that many of the soldiers destroyed themselves for fear of falling into the hands of the Bedouins. One of our battalion, who had been ill for some time, actually killed himself on a day of rest. On the pretext of cleaning his musket he went down to the river side and blew out his brains.

From this point we turned back by the same route, across the bridge and along the left bank of the Schellif, and then following the foot of the mountains, we resumed our incendiary labours. This time, however, we were not left so entirely unmolested, for on the second day Abd-el-Kader's horsemen galloped down from the mountains and attacked the right flank and the rear of the column with so much vigour, that the general was obliged to halt several times in order to send reinforcements to the rear-guard.

Thus, with the thermometer at 100°, in a plain entirely bare of trees, the July sun darting its scorching rays full upon our heads, we had to return the incessant fire of the Bedouins, enveloped in the smoke and flames of the burning corn, and without a drop of water to quench our thirst! Truly, if purgatory be half so hot one year's penance would suffice to wipe out more sins than I have committed in all my life.

The Bedouins pursued us as far as the eastern boundary of the plain, where they left us by degrees. The number of the sick had increased so terribly that the general now resolved to send them to

Blidah, and then to march with the rest of the column into the mountains of Cherchell. Among the sick was the Duke of Aumale, who had been carried in a litter for several days, and, indeed, this was probably the true reason for sending the sick to the hospital. General Bedeau, who had been made *Maréechal-de-Camp* during this expedition, commanded the convoy of sick. The Duke of Aumale[1] succeeded General Bedeau in the command of the 17th Light regiment, which had distinguished itself most honourably in every expedition.

From this point the column marched to Medeah in one day, a distance of at least sixteen leagues. We stayed two days in that town to rest the weary soldiers.

Our cavalry had the good fortune to surprise a hostile tribe concealed in a neighbouring valley, and to take a great number of cattle. On leaving Medeah we crossed the main ridge of the lesser Atlas to the westward of the Col de Mussaia, through some defiles which took the whole day to pass. We had not, however, such a height to climb as at the Col. We followed the course of a mountain torrent which forms several considerable waterfalls. The heights on either side were covered with the finest pine and olive trees, and the whole scene was wildly beautiful.

We reached the northern slope of the lesser Atlas on the second evening, and bivouacked in a small olive grove. Directly after midnight our cavalry started in deep silence, and the rest of the column followed before daybreak. We marched westward into the mountains, between Milianah and Cherchell, the abode of several considerable Kabyle tribes, among which the Beni-Manasser is the most powerful. We marched very rapidly, only halting ten or fifteen minutes at a time, till four o'clock p. m., when we heard several shots just before us, which re-echoed a thousand times among the high mountains.

As we concluded that our cavalry were already engaged with the hostile tribes, we hastened our march, and were soon met in a valley by a tribe of Kabyles,—men, women, and children, and countless herds of cattle, flying before our cavalry. After a short resistance, most of the men able to bear arms,—some on horseback, and some on foot,—fled in all directions, and hid themselves in the mountains. The old men, women and children, and twelve or fifteen thousand head of

---

1. The Duke of Aumale has since made his entry into Paris at the head of this regiment. 'Tis a pity that it was not then in the same plight to which it was reduced by this expedition, that the Parisians might have formed some idea of what the war in Africa really is.

beasts, consisting of sheep, goats, two thousand cows, and a few camels, fell into our hands. Many of the goats had four horns.

As our bivouac was not far from some Kabyle villages, we of course went to look at them. They lay almost hidden at the foot of the mountains, and high hedges of prickly pear surrounded and nearly concealed from sight the low huts built of rough stone, and covered with a flat roof of rushes. Most of these hovels had already been set on fire by our cavalry. Some of the soldiers searched the burning huts at the peril of their lives, but found nothing save a few sheep skins, a pot of honey, and some cats, who seemed unwilling to leave their homes.

We made a sortie on each of the two following days, but came too late on both. The tribes were informed of what had happened, and we found nothing but their empty huts.

The prisoners, chiefly old men, women and children, were driven with the cattle, under a special guard, in the middle of the column; it was heart-rending to see women and children, unaccustomed to walking and barefooted, compelled to follow the rapid march of the column, over rocks and briars. Their feet were soon torn and bleeding, and they dragged themselves along with the greatest difficulty. They seldom made any complaint: only when one of their number dropped from fatigue, and was left behind, they all uttered a loud wail.

We now left the mountain and turned back towards the plains of the Metidja, where we encountered all the horrors of an African summer. Every trace of vegetation had disappeared; the burning sun had so parched the soil that it was full of clefts large enough for a man to hide in. The dark green of the few scattered olive trees was changed to a dirty yellow; in short, a northern winter with its snowy mantle, is a cheering sight when compared to the desert and melancholy aspect of an African summer.

During the summer months the nights are as cold as the days are hot; the change of temperature is felt at sunset, and towards daybreak a heavy dew falls, as penetrating as rain, and very dangerous to the health; it frequently produces diseases of the eyes which end in blindness. The natives invariably draw their *bernouses* over their heads at night to protect them from the bad effects of the dew; we have adopted this custom, and the soldiers seldom lie down at night without a cap or a handkerchief over their faces.

We marched towards Blidah across the plain at the foot of the Sahel mountains. This ridge of the chain is low at this point; it is highest near Algiers. It contains most beautiful and fruitful vales, in which are forsaken gardens and villas which once belonged to the Moors. The heights are covered with dwarf oaks and other shrubs which shelter numbers of wild boars, smaller and less fierce than those of Europe: the soldiers often kill them with their bayonets. The natives assert that the Spaniards brought these unclean animals into the country out of spite. As swine are an abomination to the Mahomedan, and may not be eaten, the breed increasss rapidly. The strongest expression of contempt that an Arab can use to an European is "*Haluf.*" (swine).

At about three leagues from Coleah, on some high table land in the Sahel mountains, stands a gigantic African monument, which both the Arab and the French call the Queen's Tomb. It is in the form of a *marabout*, built of rough stone, and has every appearance of great antiquity. The natives attach the following legend to it. Once upon a time a Spanish queen landed on this coast with an army of fifty thousand men, in order to conquer the country; but even at her landing an evil omen foretold her failure: as she left her vessel the crown fell from her head into the sea, and could never be found again.

A great battle was fought on the very spot where the *marabout* now stands, the queen was beaten and destroyed with her whole army, and the tomb was raised by the Arabs as a memorial of their victory. The Arabs still seek the lost crown on this coast, and it is said that from time to time pearls of prodigious size and beauty are found upon the beach. Some of the better informed among the Arabs have told me that the monument contains graves of the Numidian kings, which seems rather more probable: at any rate it is of high antiquity. Nor do I remember to have read of any Spanish or other queen who ever invaded this country.

Not very far from Blidah, we came upon several French regiments of the line bivouacking on the plain, and at work upon a ditch and breastwork which the governor had commanded to be thrown up the whole way from the sea to Blidah,—a distance of ten leagues,—in order to protect the Metidja from the attacks of the Bedouins. The ditch is about ten feet deep by twenty wide, with a breastwork in proportion, strengthened with palisades; small blockhouses are built at intervals of a thousand paces to command the ditch.

This work will very much impede, if it does not totally prevent, the nocturnal forays of the Bedouins; it will, at any rate, put a stop to their coming on horseback, and in great troops. If a few should even steal in on foot between the blockhouses, they would not be able to drive away their prey, such as cattle, &c., which is their chief object.

The completion of this eighth wonder of the world is much to be desired, for the protection of the lives and properties of the unfortunate colonists in the plain, and as an inducement to others to settle there, for colonisation has made very little progress hitherto. Buffarik, a small village chiefly inhabited by Germans, is the only colony in the plain.

Coleah, Duera, and Delia Ibrahim are the only colonies of any importance in the Sahel, and even there the whole colonisation consists of *cafés*, canteens, and a few kitchen gardens.

At Coleah they have begun to form a colony of old worn out soldiers, but I have great doubts of its success. These veterans, it is true, have the double advantage of being tolerably well used to the climate and of knowing how to conduct themselves with prudence and coolness when attacked by the enemy; on the other hand, an old soldier generally makes a very bad peasant, and is ten times more patient of the dangers and hardships of war than of daily work with spade and plough. He usually takes unto himself some profligate woman not at all likely to attach him to his home, and then of course, neglects his farm, and soon dissipates the small sum allowed him by the government, and the end of it all is, that he sells his oxen and his plough, turns off his female companion and enlists for a few years more. And now the old fellow who used to curse the service heartily, finds it quite a decent and comfortable way of life, and it is amusing to hear with what indignation he speaks of the life of a colonist.

The only means of establishing a permanent colony in Africa would be for the French government to send over, at some expense it is true, a number of real agricultural families from the north of France, or, better still, from Germany. The southern Frenchmen are totally unfit for colonists. The only kind of agriculture which they would be able to pursue with any profit is the cultivation of the grape, and this is strictly prohibited, for fear of injuring the mother country. Hitherto the government never seems to have been really in earnest about the colonisation of Africa.

The column returned to Algiers through Blidah, Buffarik, and Duera. From Algiers we are to be distributed into summer quarters: winter quarters do not exist here. One battalion is to be sent, for the present, to Mustapha Superieur, the *depôt* of the Foreign Legion; and we shall soon go to Coleah, a town in the Sahel mountains, in a most healthy situation, to recruit after our fatigues and losses.

Chapter 7

Hôpital du Dey

Algiers, September, 1841.

Our regiment has lain eight days under the walls of Algiers, between the Casabah and *Fort l'Empereur,* on the very highest point of the whole town. Some wooden sheds have been assigned to us as quarters.

We marched hither from Coleah in two days without great exertion: and are in daily expectation of embarking to join the column at Mostaganem.

A few clays ago our regiment was inspected by the Military *Intendant* and the Inspector-General, whose duty it is to examine the state of the troops every three months: but as we have been constantly in active service, this is the first time since I have joined the Legion that a review has taken place. These officers are supposed to assure themselves that the troops and materials of war are in efficient condition, and to see that the men have everything to which they are entitled. The whole affair is however a mere formality. The two gentlemen walk through the ranks, look at the reports, and ask here and there a soldier whether he has any complaints to make: after which they get into their carriage, complimenting the commander in the most flattering terms, on the admirable condition of his regiment.

Reclamations made by the soldiers are satisfied in the most summary manner by arrest for groundless complaints. There is unfortunately often cause enough for complaint in all the regiments, but the means of appeal are so complicated that a soldier has the greatest difficulty in making his grievance known. Any commissioned or noncommissioned officer who ventured to assist him would never be forgiven, and must give up all hopes of advancement as long as he lives. Nothing is so odious to the French as a *reclameur.*

I do not think that the Military *Intendants* answer the purpose for which they were intended,—that of preventing abuses. If the soldiers have no confidence in their superior officers, they will have still less in these *intendants*, who are not at all more infallible, and who in case of any abuse only go shares with the former. At all events the *intendants* are universally hated by the soldiers. They are generally sent here by favour and protection, to recruit their broken fortunes; as the Roman *Praetors* and *Proconsuls* were sent into the conquered provinces. They know nothing of the soldiers, and care nothing about them. That their office is a very lucrative one, is sufficiently proved by the luxurious lives which most of them lead. A *harem* of women of all nations, balls and dinners, compensate these gentlemen for the want of the Parisian *salons*.

I walked to the great hospital called *l'Hôpital du Dey* to visit a sick friend. This building stands on the western side of the city, in the gardens formerly belonging to the *Dey*, and its position on the slope of the Sahel, open to the refreshing sea breeze, is equally healthy and delightful. The *Dey's* palace is converted into apartments for sick officers, and for those connected with the administration of the hospital, while as many as fifty or sixty wooden sheds have been erected in the vast garden, and constitute the actual hospital. These are capable of containing eight thousand men, and yet they are sometimes insufficient for the number of sick who pour in from all sides. They are well built and provided with beds, but not solid enough to keep out the heat of summer.

The treatment and care of the patients are not bad for Africa. The soldiers, indeed, complain that they are starved, and that all their diseases are doctored with rice water and *tisane*; but these are good remedies for diarrhoea and fevers, which are the prevailing disorders. Besides, discontent is one of the characteristics of the soldier. At any rate, the hospitals are much improved since Bugeaud's arrival. In several places they have begun to build strong massive hospitals, to replace the wooden sheds; and the frequent personal visits of the governor have done much towards abolishing the prevailing abuses and the rough treatment of the surgeons.

With considerable difficulty I found my friend, who was already convalescent; as he was just starting for a walk along the winding paths of the garden, I accompanied him. Everything had been done here to satisfy the southern longing after shade and water. Earthen pipes conveyed the freshest water the whole way from the mountains to various parts of the garden in which it gushed forth, and thick winding alleys of magnificent orange and almond trees afforded the most refreshing shade. All the sick who were able to leave their beds were assembled in these shady walks enjoying the cool sea breeze; this host of ghostlike beings crawling slowly along in their grey capotes and white night-caps had a most singular appearance; their glazed eyes looked sadly out of their sallow emaciated faces, all of which bore traces of misery, and most of melancholy and homesickness.

It was easy to guess the character and station of the invalids from the nature of their conversation or amusements. Some lay on the ground playing at cards or with dice: these were old veterans who had long given up all idea of a peaceable domestic life, and whose only object was to kill time. Others walked up and down relating their ex-ploits and occasionally criticizing their generals and officers;—these still had a remnant of enthusiasm for their calling. Others again sat on the benches around with drooping heads, and talked of their homes and of the mistresses they had left behind. Several times I heard the mournful exclamation, "*Ma belle France!*" Poor devils! many of them will never see fair France again.

I took leave of my friend with a melancholy feeling, methought I had, like Odysseus, gone down living into the world of shadows.

CHAPTER 8

Voyage to Mostaganem

Mostaganem, October, 1841.

On the 4th instant our battalion went on board a brig-of-war, of fourteen guns, which was to take us from Algiers to Mostaganem. We sailed under the most favourable auspices: a gentle easterly breeze filled our sails and we soon lost sight of Algiers. At noon we passed La Torre Chica where the French landed in 1830, and from whence they marched upon Algiers. It is the best landing-place on the whole coast. Towards evening when we were nearly opposite Cherchell the wind fell and was succeeded by a dead calm which lasted all night. The night was such as can only be seen and felt on the Mediterranean: the air was so warm that I could not endure the heat between decks, and accordingly brought up my blanket and lay down upon deck. The sky was deep blue and the stars seemed larger and nearer to me than I had ever seen them before. The ship floated like a nutshell on the boundless and glassy surface of the sea.

This ominous calm was followed by a fearful storm. The day broke with the most threatening appearances: the sun rose blood-red and evidently with no good intentions. Is umbers of sea fowl gathered round the ship screeching with hunger; a quantity of small fish sprang terror-stricken out of the water, in which they were pursued by the larger ones; and on reaching the surface they were instantly devoured by the gulls: for even the brute creation acknowledges but one right— that of the strongest. In the distance we saw a shoal of porpoises tumbling head over heels towards the south-west. These signs made the old sailors shake their heads and prophecy a bad night;—nor were they deceived.

Towards evening we saw the sea heaving from the south-west, as if urged by some unknown power. The captain ordered the sails to be shortened, and at the shrill whistle of the boatswain some twenty sailors ran up the rigging. The top-sails were scares reefed before the storm was upon us. The ship reeled so much under the shock of the gale that our masts nearly touched the water: a loud crack was suddenly heard, and one of the sails flew like a seagull through the air; the bolt-ropes had given way. The good ship now righted. In a moment all but a try-sail was made snug, and the head of the vessel was turned to meet the blast.

We retreated before the beating waves, but only step by step, like a brave warrior. By this time night had closed in with a sky as dark and dreary as old chaos; the sea alone was bright and clear, as if the better to show its yawning depths. At one moment the ship hovered on the top of a towering wave, and at the next she plunged so deep that the first rolling wave threatened to swallow us up.

I leaned against the mast, holding by a rope for fear of being washed overboard, entranced by the sight of the raging sea, and astonished at its beauty. Beautiful as is the sea in repose, it is far more beautiful in anger. The calm fills us with dreary melancholy, while the storm inspires us with the full feeling of our own power and activity. In such moments as these I never think of danger.

On the following morning we saw the Balearic Isles just behind us, and were losing ground. The dark olive woods of the island of Majorca rose higher and higher out of the sea, and we had the agreeable prospect of becoming very closely acquainted with the jagged rocky shore of the island, and of trying the hardness of our skulls against that of its stones.

Most fortunately the storm somewhat abated, and the wind veered round to the northward, so that we could set a few of our sails and steer our old course towards Mostaganem.

Although the north wind favoured us, we made very little way that day, as the sea ran very high from the south-west and the ship laboured violently and was tossed like a ball on the ocean. During the night the sea went down a little, and we continued our course with a moderate north-wind.

One of our battalion died this morning: the body was lashed upon a board and lowered into the sea without further ceremony. "*Vois tu, Pierre, comme il nous regarde*," said an old sailor to one of his messmates, pointing to the already distant corpse.

"To be sure," answered the other "they all do so as long as the ship is in sight." I looked after him, and true enough, each time the dead man rose and sunk with the waves, he turned his pale face towards the vessel. No class of men are more superstitious than sailors, unless indeed it be soldiers.

Towards evening we saw the coast of Mostaganem, and on the top of a high rock the town with its fort and surrounding blockhouses. Mostaganem has no proper harbour, only a roadstead which cannot be used except in calm weather. It was night when we cast anchor, and as the sea was then smooth and might possibly become rough, the captain sent us ashore in his boats. As he was assisted in this operation by several larger boats which came from the shore, the battalion was soon landed. It was too late to march up to the town, so we took up our well-known quarters in the *Hôtel à la Belle Etoile*. Our bed was soon made; everyone wrapped himself as well as he could in his blanket, laid his head on his knapsack, and was soon lulled to sleep by the regular murmur of the waves.

In a short time I woke again; the deepest silence reigned around me, and the stars looked down upon me as bright and calm and cheerful as if they had never known grief, nor troubled themselves in the least about the miseries of the unfortunate dwellers upon earth. The solemn silence of nature was only broken by the chafing of the waves against the rocks. I lay and watched wave after wave break at my feet, till I gradually sunk into a most pleasing reverie. In spite of all the hardships and distresses it has inflicted upon me,—in spite of sea biscuit and sea sickness, I still love the sea. When a boy, my secret and favourite scheme was to build me a castle on the sea shore, therein to end my days, and at last to die like the king of Thule:

There drank the old carouser
His last—last spirit's glow,
Then flung the hallowed wine cup
Down to the flood below.

He saw it falling, filling.
And sinking in the main;
For him—his eyes were sinking—
He never drank again.[1]

That was indeed a jovial and glorious death! I could not wish a better.

---

1. I have borrowed these lines from a translation of Goethe's well-known ballad, *Der König in Thule*, by the Rev. Dr. Hawtrey, published in his *Auswahl von Goethe's Lyrischen Gedichten.*—Trans.

After daybreak we marched to Mostaganem, which stands half a league from the sea, and took up our quarters in some wooden sheds under the walls of Matamor.

Matamor is a small Moorish fort built on a rock commanding the town. Here the Spaniards formerly won a great victory over the Moors, and thence the name *Matamoros* (kill the Moors).

Mostaganem is separated from this fort by a considerable brook, which rises at about two leagues up the mountain. The town is accessible only from the south, by one solitary gate; on every other side it is surrounded by a deep ravine at the bottom of which roars a mountain torrent, or by lofty and precipitous walls of rock. It would therefore seem easy enough to defend Mostaganem against any attack, but unfortunately Fort Matamor, which should protect the town, itself needs protection, as it is commanded by a neighbouring height, and its walls are not of sufficient strength to resist heavy ordnance; and thus it was that the French obtained possession first of the fort and subsequently of the town.

Mostaganem contains four or five thousand inhabitants, Arabs, Spaniards and Jews, besides the French regiment in garrison. The town must formerly have been much larger, as is shown by the number of ruins scattered without the walls; but, with the exception of a few mosques, there is no building of any importance. The former citadel, the Casabah, is in ruins, and is only garrisoned by some fifty or sixty pairs of storks who have founded a colony on the extensive walls.

Almost as much Spanish is spoken here as French or Arabic. Nearly all the natives speak a corrupt Spanish, a kind of *lingua franca*, which prevails in all the towns on the coast of Africa. The younger generation, however,—boys from 10 to 14—speak French with tolerable fluency, but somewhat marred by their deep guttural tone. The ease with which Arabs and Bedouins continue to imitate whatever they have but once seen or heard is very remarkable. Nature seems to have bestowed this gift of imitation on half-savage nations to compensate them for the want of original invention.

The general lives in the town, where some of the best houses have been arranged for him and his staff; the troops are quartered in wooden sheds, partly in the town and partly under the walls of Matamor. These sheds would hold as many as fifteen thousand men, but the actual number is nine thousand, including the allied cavalry, which is composed of from two to three thousand Arabs and Bedouins under the command of a native leader, called the *Bey* of Mostaganem. He is a fine handsome man of about forty, and was formerly a friend and devoted adherent of Abd-el-Kader, in which capacity he gave the French much trouble. He once proposed to Abd-el-Kader to make an attempt to recover his lost town of Mascara which, the French had taken and then left, ill provisioned and worse garrisoned: the *emir* did not enter into the scheme with sufficient alacrity to please the *Bey* who denounced Abd-el-Kader as a coward, and threatened to desert him and to join the French.

This was no sooner said than done. He and his two or three thousand horsemen went over to the French, and he has been their most faithful ally ever since. The general treats him with the greatest distinction, and his own people reverence him as a prince. He never goes out without a considerable suite; on his left rides a *marabout*, and on his right the officer whose duty is to shelter him from the sun with a huge yellow umbrella; he is preceded by musicians beating the *tam tam*, a large drum, accompanied by pipes and cymbals. They always play the same tune, which seems to be a triumphal march, discordant enough to European ears, but delightful to Arab ones.

The moment the *tam tam* sounds, the Arabs rock themselves to and fro in their saddles with pleasure; and I must confess, that diabolical as I thought this music at first, I grew fond of it in time, and something seemed wanting to me if the Arab march was not played on entering or leaving the bivouac; so true is it that old familiar tunes affect us most powerfully. Most likely it is less the music itself than the crowd of images and recollections which it awakens in our minds that exercises such magic power over us. For this reason every regiment should have a march of its own, to be played on particular occasions, as is the case with most regiments here. When the well-known tones of the regimental march strike upon the ear of the weary and exhausted men, the effect is magical: their wan faces brighten up, their muscles acquire fresh strength, and they march forwards with renewed vigour, perhaps even humming a song.

It is said that the French government pays the *Bey* as much as forty thousand *francs* a year for his services. Each Arab soldier receives a *franc* a day, out of which he has to maintain himself and his horse; besides this pay he has his share of the *razzia* money. The booty made on these expeditions is distributed, or should be so legally, among the officers and soldiers according to their rank; but the common soldiers complain, and perhaps not quite without reason, that the higher powers are apt to keep the lion's share for themselves. The *Bey* and the superior officers lodge in the town; the rest of the Arab cavalry is encamped without the walls on the southern side of the brook.

Each soldier has his own tent, where his wife or wives manage his household; his horse stands picketed and usually ready saddled at his door, both summer and winter. A few minutes suffice to prepare this body of cavalry for action. At the sight of the colours flying on the top of the mosque, and at the sound of the *tam tam*, the Arabs jump on their horses and follow their leader.

A few days ago a report was suddenly spread that Abd-el-Kader had seized our cattle at pasture in a valley about a league hence; the general march was beat, the colours were hoisted on the top of the mosque, and the warlike *tam tam* was sounded. In one moment all were under arms, and each division marched as it was ready: the Arabs started off singly and galloped to the scene of action, spurring their bleeding horses to their utmost speed; they swung their long rifles round their heads as if they had been javelins, crying aloud, "*Phantasia! Phantasia!*" in their joy and eagerness for battle. It is not possible to conceive a wilder or more beautiful picture of war. Before we could reach the spot, panting and heated from running, the action was over. Our herds and their guards had been attacked by a few bold robbers belonging to a neighbouring tribe, who had fled at the approach of our Arab cavalry: a chase ensued, but without success, for the robbers were as well mounted as their pursuers, and had a considerable start and no inconsiderable fear in their favour.

Most of our Arab horsemen are mounted on Bedouin horses, which are a neglected variety of the Barbary breed; they are small and lean, but of wonderful speed and endurance: with very short intervals of rest they can keep up a sort of long gallop up and down hill, over any sort of broken ground for the whole day, and they are as sure-footed as goats.

The Arabs ride with matchless boldness down the precipitous and broken sides of the mountains. Often, when we have been pursued by the enemy and left them as we thought on the very top of the mountain, in a few minutes we have been astonished by their bullets whistling about our ears.

Besides the *Bey's* horsemen, several considerable tribes of Arabs and Bedouins near Mostaganem and Oran have submitted to the French, and come daily to the town with their camels and horses to bring fruit, corn, vegetables, cattle, &c., to market. They cannot fail to discover in time that they derive the most solid advantages from the French dominion, under which their lives and properties are far more secure than they ever were before, and their produce is trebled in value. The latter circumstance they are especially able to appreciate, for, barbarians as they are, they well know the value of money; indeed, I never saw men so rapacious as the Bedouins; perhaps their avarice is called forth by the contact with Europeans.

It is highly entertaining to see the soldiers haggling with the Bedouins for fruit, eggs, &c. The soldier comes with the full intention of overreaching the Bedouin (*lui tirer une carotte*), and of robbing him by force or fraud, of a fowl or of some eggs, for in Africa everything is a lawful prize. The Bedouin, on the other hand, who most likely has been cheated two or three times before, stands resolutely on the defensive and never parts with anything until the money is paid into his hand. This provokes abuse, in which, however, the Bedouin far excels even the Frenchman, and blows not unfrequently follow; but the Bedouin would rather lose his life than the smallest fraction of his property, and the fight continues till a *sergent de police* comes up and puts an end to it.

The hundreds of Bedouins mounted on camels and horses, and the quantity of Arab cavalry interspersed with soldiers in various uniforms, give a very peculiar air to Mostaganem. It is a perfect picture of a camp, where in spite of want, misery, and of danger past, present, and future, the childish, careless joyousness of the soldiers is everywhere apparent.

About a league from here is Fort Massagran, famous for the heroic defence by Captain Lièvre. I have heard an account of this whole affair from eye-witnesses, and am fully persuaded that the defence was one of the most gallant actions of the whole war, although it was somewhat exaggerated by the French newspapers. The fort, the walls of which are tolerably high and strong, stands on a *plateau* which falls precipitously on the northern side, rendering the fort inaccessible in that quarter. The village of Massagran lies somewhat lower down and could only be defended indirectly.

Captain Lievre had under him a hundred and fifty *disciplinaires* and a few cannon, while for several days in succession the fort was assailed by a host of six or eight thousand Bedouins, on foot and on horseback, who made several attempts to carry the place by storm. All their attacks were repulsed with the most determined coolness, until at length the fort was relieved by troops sent from Mostaganem. It is true that the garrison had the advantage of high walls and some artillery, but anyone who knows how powerfully so overwhelming a mass of assailants affects men's minds, can estimate the extraordinary experience and intrepidity required in order to retain thorough .self-possession. The whole company of *disciplinaires* who had formed the garrison, were immediately reinstated among the regiments of the line, and each soldier received a medal struck for the occasion. Captain Lièvre was made a *Commandant* and received the cross of the Legion of Honour.

Commandant Lièvre has the reputation of a brave and distinguished officer; he commanded a battalion of the Fifty-Third regiment, (if I am not mistaken,) which formed part of our *colonne mobile*, and of almost every expedition up to July 1842.[2]

Mostaganem and Oran have been for centuries the ports to which all the caravans from the interior of Africa have come to exchange their produce with that of the north. The towns of Mascara and Tlemcen, which are but a few days' march from hence, served them as resting-places and warehouses; and they have lost the source of their wealth and importance since the French occupation has driven the caravan trade to Morocco.

The district south of Mostaganem may be called the home of the Bedouins, if indeed these wanderers have a home. There the richest and most powerful tribes fix their tents, sow and reap their corn, and feed their flocks, purposes for which the country is well adapted. The large plains between Mostaganem, Mascara, and Oran, and the fertile valleys of the Schellif and the Mina, afford these nomads excellent pasture for their numerous herds, and an unlimited run for their horses and camels. During the whole winter, and till the month of June, which is their harvest time, the Bedouins camp in these places; but when the heat has burnt up whatever pasture was left, they retreat into the valleys and defiles of the Atlas, where food of some sort, though scanty, is still to be found for their flocks and herds.

Many of the tribes near Mostaganem and Oran have submitted to the French; thanks to the zeal and activity of General Lamoricière, the governor of the province of Oran. They prefer paying a moderate tribute and feeding their herds in peace, to seeing their property, their wives and their children continually exposed to the unexpected attack

---

2. I saw, at Paris, a caricature of the defence of Massagran. A hare, in full uniform, stands on the walls in the act of devouring several Bedouins; thousands more are at the foot of the wall, filled with horror and amazement at this unheard-of proceeding. Underneath is written—*"Le Lièvre est un fameux lapin."*

of a *colonne mobile.*

Middle of October.

Nature is just beginning to shake off the lethargy produced by the deadly, parching heat of summer. A few rainy days are sufficient to call into existence, as it were by magic, the most luxuriant vegetation: the richest verdure has sprung up beneath the withered grass, the leaves of the trees have lost their sickly yellow hue, the buds have begun to burst, and the birds to sing their spring songs. In short, this is the African spring, but I must assert my preference for the real spring in Germany.

The revival of nature in the north is more powerful and all-pervading, though not so sudden. In a northern climate every creature greets with a more heartfelt gratitude the glorious freshness and beauty of the woods and fields when their icy winter clothing has been stripped off by the returning sun. A more joyful thrill runs through us when the first lark rises towards heaven, pouring out its shrill hymn of praise, and the confiding swallow builds her nest under the eaves of our houses. It is far different here: it is true the song of the birds still pleases me, and the green carpet of nature is refreshing to my eyes. But not as in Europe. It may be, indeed, that the change does not lie in nature but in myself: the experience of a few hard years has, perhaps, blunted my feelings, and made me less capable of enjoying her beauties.

The burst of vegetation was strongest in the valley which divides the fort from the town, and which is watered by a stream. Every inch of ground there is turned to the profit of man: magnificent fruit trees, pomegranates, figs, and oranges, and the most various vegetables cover the ground, and Spaniards, Arabs, Jews, and Frenchmen are diligently employed in cultivating the fruitful soil. The soldier alone thinks this manual labour beneath his dignity, and lies at full length under a shady fig tree smoking a cigar and drinking his last *sou's*-worth of Spanish wine. Others are washing their shirts and gaiters at the brook: "*Mort de ma vie*" cries one; "How much better my Suzette would wash these shirts!" Another bitterly regrets the three *sous* he has expended in soap, which might have been so much better laid out on a pint of Spanish wine. These sallies produce general and joyous laughter. Poor fellows! these few days of rest and relaxation can scarce be grudged them.

The cavalry of the *Bey,* who lie at a little distance in strange, picturesque groups, form a remarkable contrast to the active, restless European soldiers. The Arab lies whole days before his tent, wrapped in his *bernouse* and leaning his head on his hand. His horse inlands ready saddled, listlessly hanging his head almost to the ground, and occasionally casting sympathising glances on his master. The African might then be supposed phlegmatic and passionless, but for the occasional flash of his wild dark eye, which gleams from under his bushy brows. His rest is like that of the Numidian lion which, when satisfied, stretches itself beneath a shady palm tree,—but beware of waking him.

Like the beasts of the desert and forest, and like all nature in his own land, the Arab is hurried from one extreme to the other,—from the deepest repose to the most restless activity. At the first sound of the *tam tam* his foot is in the stirrup, his hand on his rifle, and he is no longer the same man. He rides day and night, bears every privation, and braves every danger, in order to make a prize of some sheep, or ass, or of some enemy's head. Such men as these are hard to conquer, and harder still to govern: were they united into one people, they would form a nation which could not only repulse the French but bid defiance to the whole world. Unhappily for them every tribe is at enmity with the rest; and this must ultimately lead to their destruction, for the French have already learnt to match African against African,

The Prisoners of Abd-El-Kader
or,
Five Months' Captivity Among the Arabs

M. A. de France

CHAPTER 1.

Painful Journey

The brig *Loiret* had lain off Arzew for five months: I was serving on board this vessel commanded by Lieutenant Roland de Chabert. It is easy to conceive the dullness of our life on a desert coast devoid of all interest or amusement. Our only pleasure was a walk upon the beach, and even that was necessarily confined within the outposts, as the Arabs were incessantly lurking about the few houses which the French have built at Arzew, watching for an opportunity to carry off the cattle. They had already tried more than one *coup-de-main*, but hitherto had always been repulsed with loss.

On the 11th of August, 1836, we received orders to be ready next day, with forty of our crew, to reconnoitre a well about two leagues beyond our outposts, accompanied by part of the garrison. I was one of those selected to form part of the expedition, and went to bed at midnight, after my watch, overjoyed at the thoughts of next day's excursion up the country.

On the 12th, at four in the morning, M. Roland de Chabert, the commander of the *Loiret*, Dr. Clinchard, M. Bravois, and myself, with forty of our crew, all armed, went on shore, and found Captain Reveroni, the commandant of the place, who informed us, that General Lètang had given orders to suspend the expedition till he could send us reinforcements.

As we had made all the necessary arrangements on board for our campaign, which we expected would occupy the whole day, we determined to turn our freedom to account.

The commander and the officers of the *Loiret* proposed to go and pick up the balls, which our gunners had fired in yesterday's practice. We consulted the commandant as to the feasibility of our scheme, and the danger we might incur in going beyond the outposts. M. Reveroni approved very much of our resolution, and assured us that there would be no danger in passing the outposts, provided we did not go too far. "We accordingly took leave of M. Reveroni, and advanced into the plain: at about a hundred yards beyond the outposts we halted, and stationed some of our men on a height to give the alarm in case we were surprised by the Arabs. Having taken this precaution, we began to seek for our balls, and to measure the range of our guns; I was thus occupied, at a distance of about two musket-shots from the rest of the troop with the commander, Dr. Clinchard, and two sailors, when suddenly I espied a partridge close at hand, and after pointing it out to Dr. Clinchard, I ran after it, taking aim.

I had gone only a few steps, when a troop of Arabs suddenly poured out of a ravine, came down upon us at full gallop and surrounded us on all sides. They advanced towards me, crying, "*Semi! Semi!*" (Friends! Friends!) Deceived by these exclamations, I turned to explain them to the doctor, when one of the Arabs snatched at the musket which I held in my hand; this showed me their real intentions, and I instantly fired at the Arab who had tried to seize the musket, and broke his shoulder. He dropped his gun, which was loaded, and was forced to throw his arm round the neck of his horse to prevent falling off. I darted at the gun, but two Arabs took aim at my head, and as I turned away to avoid their fire, one ball gave me a slight wound on the head, and the other passed through my shirt and grazed my breast.

I had not lost sight of the wounded Arab's gun, and stooped again to pick it up, when something rough slipped over my face; I raised my hands to it, and felt a rope; round my neck; at the same moment, a violent jerk brought me to the ground, and an Arab, who had the other end of the rope fastened to his saddle bow, set off at full gallop.

My cries and entreaties were all in vain, the Arab spurred on his horse, and I was dragged half strangled through rocks and briars. This horrible torture lasted some minutes, until the horse was forced by steep and stony ground to slacken his pace, when I got on my feet again. In spite of the wounds with which my face, hands, and legs were covered, and the stunning effects of such a shock, I still had strength to seize the cord so as to keep myself from being strangled, and to run forward and catch hold of the horse's tail.

But as soon as the other Arabs, who had been dispersed by the sailors sent to our assistance, rejoined their companions, I was loaded with abuse and stripped nearly naked. Our misfortune had been seen from the brig, which immediately fired upon the Arabs: but every shot cost me a fresh shower of blows, and the horse to which I was tied took fright at the noise and started forward, and I again fell to the ground; the Arabs ran after me beating me all the time, and if by chance I succeeded in getting on my feet, my pitiless persecutor set off again at a gallop, casting looks of contempt upon me.

The incessant galloping of the horse and the violent jerks of the cord which dragged and rolled me among the rocks and briars, leaving a track of blood behind me—the abuse and the blows of the Arabs, lasted a quarter of an hour: this sounds but a short time, but it seemed very long to me.

As soon as the Arabs thought themselves out of reach of pursuit, they halted in order to cut off my head. The rope was taken off my neck, my hands bound behind my back, and I was tied to a dwarf palm tree. I was so tired, that I lay down upon the ground perfectly indifferent to the fate which I knew awaited all prisoners taken by the Arabs. I had but one sad thought, of my family and my poor sister, but this was soon driven away by the near approach of death and the animated scene in which I, though chained and silent, was the principal person.

A violent discussion had arisen among the Arabs: they brandished their sabres over my head, and each claimed the pleasure of cutting it off, all crying at once, "I took him, I have a right to cut off his head;" and each to prove the truth of his assertion showed a fragment of my shirt or of my coat. The Arabs were already taking aim at one another, and exclaiming, "I ought to cut off his head, and I will kill you if you don't let me enjoy my rights," when a horseman galloped up and threw into my lap the head of Jonquié, one of the sailors; as I turned away in disgust at this horrible spectacle, I saw the Arab whom I had wounded lying on the ground about fifty paces off. He could scarcely support himself, and was endeavouring to aim at me with a pistol which he held in his left hand. But horsemen were every instant passing to and fro before him, and he dropped his hand, patiently awaiting the favourable moment to fire.

I was expecting the end of this horrible discussion with some impatience, when the arrival of another horseman changed the determination of the Arabs. This was Adda, a spy of Abd-el-Kader, who had often visited us at Arzew, where he feigned an intention of establishing himself, and allayed any suspicion we might entertain of him by assuring us that his frequent visits were for the purpose of selecting some favourable spot for the settlement of his tribe. Delighted at the goodwill he manifested towards us, we had frequently invited him to dinner. But the traitor had far different designs. He made use of his visits to mark the exact spot to which our cattle were driven: he had determined to seize them, and it was with that object that he had hidden himself in the ravine with, the troop which had taken me prisoner,

When Adda saw them furiously disputing who should kill me. he exclaimed that I was an officer, and that Abd-el-Kader would give them much more for my head if it was left upon my shoulders, and would willingly replace the three horses they had lost if I were taken to him alive.

But the Arabs still continued to brandish their *yataghans* over my head, with the most horrible imprecations against the dog of a Christian.

Adda used still stronger arguments; and when the dying Arab had been removed, it was decided that I should be presented alive to Abd-el-Kader, who was to choose the manner of my death, after paying my ransom and replacing the horses which our men had shot.

I was then released from the tree, and a rope was passed through the cord which bound my arms. An Arab took hold of either end, and we started for Old Arzew.

After a march of two hours we reached Old Arzew. I was worn out with fatigue and suffering—naked, wounded, covered with dust and sweat, and dying of thirst: and I expected that my body would be left without burial at Arzew, while my head would serve to adorn Abd-el-Kader's tent.

As I was with the advanced guard of the Arabs, I was one of the first to arrive at Old Arzew. I threw myself upon the ground beside a fountain, and counted the troop which had attacked us as it defiled past me: there were about two hundred men. We halted for a quarter of an hour to rest the horses and to let the men eat a little. I was unable to swallow anything but a few figs and a little water, and had just dropped asleep when the chief gave the signal for departure, and I started under a guard of twenty-seven horsemen.

Just as we were setting off, an Arab brought me a straw hat with poor Jonquié's head in it, and bade me carry it. I refused, and was instantly assailed on all sides by blows and abuse, and cries of "Carry the head, dog of a Christian."

"I will die first," said I, throwing myself on the ground; and the Arabs were about to dispatch me with the butt ends of their rifles, when Adda, who was very anxious to deliver me alive to Abd-el-Kader, interposed. The head was hung to the saddle-bow of one of the Arabs, and after venting their ill-humour on me by more blows, we started.

During our journey across the plain of Macta, we stopped at three successive wells, where several Arabs of the neighbouring tribes met us and drew water for our men and horses. I went towards the well to drink, but the Arab who held the bucket spat in my face, saying, "This water is not for a dog of a Christian like thee."

I made no answer, and went on to the next well, but there too the Arab who was drawing water spat in my face, and said, "This water is not for a dog of a Christian like thee."

Again I bore it with patience, but the Arab at the third well, not content with spitting in my face and addressing the same compliment to me as his predecessors had done, dashed a bucket full of water in my face. I was bathed in perspiration, and no doubt such treatment would have brought on an inflammation in my chest if I had had time to be ill. As it was, I shivered and threw myself on the ground, (always my last resource,) crying "You may kill me if you please; I will not move another step, I am dying of thirst." This was no more than the truth, for my tonge and my mouth were like a piece of dry cork, and I was fainting from thirst. At length Adda went himself, drew some water and brought it to me.

We resumed our journey through a country in which the barley harvest was going on, and every time we passed any Arabs at work in the fields or a party of horsemen, my guards called out "Come and see the Christian dog;" and they all came and spat in my face, and fired off their muskets close to my head, so that the balls whizzed about my ears. I must confess that these demonstrations of joy alarmed me a good deal until I got used to them.

During the course of our day's journey we had to ford several rivers; but though I was often up to my middle in the water, these barbarians would not allow me to take a little in the palm of my hand, till at last, in spite of their threats and blows, I flung myself down in the bed of the river and drank deep draughts; this refreshed me but for a short time, and at every fresh river I had to resort to the same expedient.

At length I fell, exhausted with fatigue. It was three o'clock, and I had walked since five in the morning, and my feet were torn and bleeding. The Arabs mounted me on one of their horses, but in a quarter of an hour the owner of it dragged me off its back by my leg. I walked for two hours more, and then rode again. At length we arrived about nightfall at the camp of the Borgiá tribe.

Here I was exposed to the blows, insults, and spittings of men, women, and children. A tent was pitched for my guards into which I was but half admitted, and I lay on the earth beyond the carpet.

Our party had chickens boiled with *kuskussu* for supper, which they ate voraciously; I should have been very glad of a bit, but they considered me unworthy of such a dainty, and flung me a handful of *kuskussu*, which I could not swallow, as it was dry and bad, and my throat was so sore.

After supper the Arabs returned my shirt to me and sent a negro to put irons on my feet. My legs were so swollen that the pain of forcing the irons to shut brought tears into my eyes: this treatment was as useless as it was cruel, for I was not able to stand, much less to run away. I stretched myself on the bare ground and slept soundly till the next morning, when the brutal negro woke me by giving a violent shake to the irons on my feet, which hurt me dreadfully.

I endeavoured to rise but instantly fell again; my feet were lacerated and swollen, and all my wounds ached with cold and fatigue. The Arabs seeing that if they compelled me to walk I should soon expire by the road side, at length gave me a horse to ride, and we continued our journey towards Abd-el-Kader's camp, which was not above ten leagues off.

But for fear I should be too comfortable they hung poor Jonquié's head at my saddle-bow: it was already in a state of putrefaction, and the Arabs seeing the horror and loathing with which it inspired me, amused themselves by piercing it with their swords and *yataghans* to increase the smell by exposing the brains to the action of the sun and air.

We were travelling the road from Mascara to Mostaganem, and my heart beat for joy at the sight of the tracks of the French cannon. I hoped that we might fall in with some French outpost, and for a moment I forgot all my misery, and even the putrid and bloody head before me, and fancied myself on board the brig and in the arms of my friends and relations, or firing a broadside at the Arabs. I was rather roughly waked out of my reverie by a shower of blows which the Arabs gave me in order to hasten my horse's pace. In a few minutes I urged the animal on, and immediately they beat me violently, crying, "A Christian dog like thee may not dare to strike the horse of an Arab."

We continued our journey in this manner for six hours, at the end of which the Arabs began to shout for joy, and Adda told me that we had reached Abd-el-Kader's camp, which is close to the town of Kaala. It was not without emotion that I passed the first tents of the man who was to decide my fate.

CHAPTER 2

Arrival at Abd-el-Kader's camp

Abd-el-Kader's camp stood in a grove of fig trees, on the road from Mascara to Mostaganem, and the tracks of the wheels of the French artillery were still visible in the very midst of it. On arriving at the first tent my guards forced me to dismount, and in a moment I was surrounded by a host of Arabs of every age and both sexes, shouting and screaming—"Son of dog," "Dog of a Christian," "Cut off his head," &c., with the usual accompaniment of blows and spitting.

Presently the *chaous* came to my rescue, and by dint of vigorous blows they at last succeeded in delivering me from the hands of these savages, and conducted me to Abd-el-Kader's tent. My first reception in the camp had not been of a kind fitted to dispel the fears with which I went into his presence. But as soon as Abd-el-Kader saw the pallor of my face he smiled and motioned me to sit, saying, "As long as thou art with me fear neither insult nor ill usage."

Emboldened by this gracious reception I asked him for something to drink, as, thanks to my guards, I had not drank since the day before. Abd-el-Kader immediately ordered me to be conducted to the tent which served as a store-house, and there I received a melon, some grapes, white bread, and water. The melon was so good, the water so cool, and Abd-el-Kader's manner had been so humane, that my hopes and my appetite revived. After devouring the melon and drinking a whole jar of water, I was again led into the *Sultan's* presence.

His tent is the most magnificent in the camp: it is thirty feet long and eleven feet high; the inside is lined with hangings of various colours, covered with *arabesques* and crescents in red, blue, green, and yellow. A woollen curtain divides it into two unequal parts, in the furthermost and smaller of which is a mattress on which the *Sultan* sleeps. At the further end is a small entrance for the service of the tent and the slaves especially attached to the person of the *Sultan*: these are Ben Abu and Ben Faka, of whom I shall have to say more hereafter. During the day the tent remains open and accessible to all.

On the ground in one corner lie four silken flags rolled up: these are borne before Abd-el-Kader on every march by four horsemen; the first flag, belonging to the cavalry, is red; the second, that of the infantry, has a horizontal yellow stripe between two blue ones; the third, two horizontal stripes—one green and the other white; and the fourth is half red and half yellow. Every Friday these flags are unfurled in front of the *Sultan's* tent. There is also a small mattress covered with a carpet, on which lie two red silk cushions; at each end of the mattress is a chest, and behind it two other chests; the whole is then covered with a carpet and forms Abd-el-Kader's sofa: the chests contain his clothes and money.

A carpet is spread on the ground for strangers. These things, together with a high footstool, covered with red silk, which serves the Sultan as a horseblock, constitutes all the furniture of the *Sultan's* tent. The tent is always guarded by thirty negroes, who are never relieved and have no other bed than the earth. A good many *chaous* are always in attendance, ready to obey the commands of their ruler.

I will now endeavour to describe a man of whom at present very little is known. From all that I had heard, I expected to find a bloodthirsty barbarian, always ready to cut off heads: my expectations were false indeed.

Abd-el-Kader is twenty-eight years of age and very small, his face is long and deadly pale, his large black eyes are soft and languishing, his mouth small and delicate, and his nose rather aquiline; his beard is thin but jet black, and he wears a small *mustachio*, which gives a martial character to his soft and delicate face, and becomes him vastly. His hands are small and exquisitely formed, and his feet equally beautiful; the care he takes of them is quite *coquettish*: he is constantly washing them, and paring and filing his nails with a small knife with a beautifully-carved mother-of-pearl handle, which he holds all the while as he sits crouching on his cushions with his toes clasped between his fingers.

His dress is distinguished by the most studied simplicity; there is not a vestige of gold or embroidery on any part of it. He wears a shirt of very fine linen, the seams of which are covered with a silk braid terminating in a small silk, tassel. Over the shirt is a *haick*, and over the *haick* two white *bernouses*; the uppermost garment is a black *bernouse*.

A few silk tassels are the only ornaments about his dress; he wears no arms in his girdle, his head is shaved, and covered by three or four scull-caps one within the other, over which he draws the hood of his *bernouse*.

Abd-el-Kader's father, who died about two years ago, was a *marabout* called Mahadin, who by means of his fortune, his intelligence, and his character for sanctity, had acquired very great fame and influence among the Arabs. Twice in his life he had made the pilgrimage to Mecca, and prostrated himself before the tomb of the Prophet. In his second journey he was accompanied by his son, who was but eight years old. Young as he was, Abd-el-Kader acquired a great deal of useful experience, and learned Italian: he could already read and write Arabic. After returning from their pious journey, Mahadin instructed his son in the difficult study of the *Koran*, and at the same time taught him the conduct of affairs.

As soon as we had concluded a peace with the Arabs after the taking of Algiers, Abd-el-Kader employed himself in exciting the tribes to revolt, in feeding and exasperating their animosity towards us, in stirring up their religious fanaticism, and above all in endeavouring to obtain the sovereign power over them. This, the talent, the energy, the bravery, and the cunning of the young *marabout* soon procured for him; he quickly became their chief, and is now their *Sultan*.

The second time that I went to the *Sultan's* tent he was seated on some cushions with his secretaries and some *marabouts* crouching in a semicircle on either side of him: his smiling and graceful countenance contrasted charmingly with the stupid savage faces around him. The chief secretary first attracted my attention by his *Tartuffe* expression, and the rogue has always persuaded Abd-el-Kader to ask a large sum for my ransom.

The *Sultan*, with a smile of the greatest kindness, bade me be seated, and asked me, in Arabic, my name and where I was taken, and on my answering his questions, told me to fear nothing so long as I was with him.

He then began to talk about our generals who have commanded in Africa, and was very curious to know what had become of them all. On hearing the name of General Trézel, he flew into a violent rage, and cried, "He was author of all our misfortunes; it was he who broke the peace and caused such endless disasters!" I saw that he alluded to the Battle of Tafna, by which General Bugeaud made up for the defeat at Macta, where we lost five hundred men.

"How many horsemen did you lose at Tafna?" asked I.

"How many?" cried he, furiously. "How many? What is that to thee? The Arabs were not killed at Tafna as the French were at Macta; you have never retrieved my great victory over you there. Five hundred of our men did not return from Tafna."

Now as the Arabs are the greatest liars in the world, one may fairly presume that General Bugeaud killed at least twelve hundred of them at Tafna; but I took very good care to make no further remark; and after a few moments of silence the *Sultan* smiled again and said—

"Dost thou desire anything more today?"

"I am quite naked, give me some clothes," said I, and immediately, at a sign from Abd-el-Kader, I was taken to the store tent and furnished with a scull-cap, a very thin *haick*, a shirt, and a pair of slippers: my trowsers were also returned to me and I put them on, though all in rags, as no others were to be had.

No sooner was I dressed, than I was accosted by a man, or rather a phantom, wrapped in a ragged *haick*, pale and emaciated, with a long uncombed beard, naked chest and meagre legs, and every appearance of having endured long and cruel misery; a smile lit up his wan dejected countenance as he said—

"Don't you recognise me. Sir?"

"No, Sir, I am not aware that I ever saw you before," said I.

"Oh, that is because I have suffered so much since we met. I hear that you are a prisoner, and for your sake I am very sorry for it, for you do not yet know all the torments that await you; but I cannot conceal from you the joy your presence gives me. I shall no longer be alone; I shall have a companion who will share my sufferings, and to whom I can talk of my country and of my sorrows, and I shall suffer less. But have you really forgotten me, M. de France? I met you at dinner at M. Lafont's."

"At M. Lafont's? Good heavens! are you M. Meurice?"

The unfortunate man wrung my hand, and his eyes filled with tears. I said everything I could think of to encourage and cheer him; but while I talked hopefully and gladly, my thoughts were occupied with poor Meurice's wretched appearance: his face disfigured by pain, his extreme thinness, the feebleness of his limbs, and the dejection of his spirits, gave me the idea of a dying man. When I saw him at M. Lafont's dinner at Algiers, he was a stout healthy man of about forty, good-looking, lively, and agreeable; but ill-usage and suffering had stupefied him, destroyed all his energy and powers of mind, and unhinged his whole frame; he was now weak, credulous, almost imbecile, he had endured unheard-of tortures which I had escaped, and he had not, like me, been inured to hardships and privations by a sailor's life.

The tent in which we were lodged was as large as that of Abd-el-Kader, but not nearly so handsome: it served as a general magazine for victuals and ammunition. Near it was another which was used as the *Sultan's* kitchen, and where, besides, all the barley and *kuskussu* for the troops was kept. A third tent contained all sorts of military stores and clothing, and the provisions of oil and butter.

An old negro, called Ben Faka, was the governor of our tent: he was formerly a slave of Abd-el-Kader's father; he has known the *Sultan* from his birth, and is extremely attached to him; with us he would be called the Commissary General.

The *Sultan's* treasurer is Ben Abu his old tutor: he has the care of Abd-el-Kader's tent and treasure during the battle, and enjoys his entire confidence. Ben Abu stammers, owing to a shot which carried away half his teeth and half his tongue. He and Ben Faka are charged with the especial care of the *Sultan's* person. The commander of the troops is called Milud-ben-Arrach: he is always grave and solemn, and never smiles. His lieutenant is an Arab called Muftar. who has especial command over the horse. During the peace Muftar frequently came to Oran, where he saw the manoeuvres of the French cavalry, and he has been trying ever since to discipline his Arabs in the same manner but totally without success, as the Arabs can never understand the possibility of keeping the line while charging at full speed.

I took care to impress the features of these different officers on my memory, in the hope that I might one day have an opportunity of repaying them their blows, insults, and odious persecutions with lashes, and the most cruel among them with bullets.

The *Sultan* has in his camp about two hundred and fifty horsemen and five hundred foot soldiers, who are paid and clothed at his expense; among the Arabs the cavalry are lodged in the centre of the camp, surrounded and guarded by the infantry. The *califah*, or general-in-chief, is encamped near Tlemsen with as many more, and it is with this handful of men that Abd-el-Kader drives all the neighbouring tribes to battle.

CHAPTER 3

Meurice's Story

Meurice begged me to give him an account of my capture and subsequent adventures. I had just finished it, and requested to hear his story in return, when a negro brought us some *kuskussu* for supper. It was quite dark, and he lit a taper of yellow wax, about the size of a farthing rush-light, stuck it on a bit of stick which he poked into the earth, and bade us lie down. We stretched ourselves upon the bare ground and the negro went away.

I wish I were as well skilled in the management of my pen as in that of a vessel, so that I might be able to bring vividly before my readers a picture of the dark savage tent filled with strange-looking packages, and in it the two prisoners lying on the ground; Meurice, pale and livid, with his long matted beard and dim eyes, telling in a sad and weary voice, the unhappy adventure which had suddenly snatched him from a life of case and enjoyment, and plunged him into the most frightful and degrading misery. I will give his story, as nearly as I can remember, in his own words.

"I was compelled," said he, "to leave Paris after the Revolution of 1830, by losses in trade. I settled at Algiers with my young wife, and exercised the profession of a land surveyor, in which I had plenty of employment. My life, though rather monotonous, was very agreeable, thanks to Clarissa's incessant attentions to my comfort, and to her charming disposition. Poor thing! she is so pretty, so amiable, you shall read her letters. Alas! perhaps I may never see her again.

"On the 20th of April, 1836, I had been to inspect an estate near the Metidja. and was returning in company with M. Muller, a civil engineer, M. D—— and his sister. I was on horseback, M. Muller on a mule, and M. and Mile. D—— in a carriage.

"On a sudden we were surrounded by a troop of Arabs: we were all totally unarmed, except M. D——, who had a gun; but he was so terrified, that without even firing it off he darted out of the carriage, took to his heels and hid himself in a marsh, where the horsemen could not follow him. M. Muller received a ball in his thigh which hurt him severely, and was instantly taken prisoner. The Arabs next seized Mlle. D—— and endeavoured to force her to comply with their brutal desires, but threats, blows, and pistols held to her breast, failed to overcome her heroic resistance, and the noble girl was actually cut to pieces before our eyes without uttering a single cry.

"The Arabs dragged M. Muller and myself away with them, but were soon obliged to leave M. Muller behind with the Hadjutes, seeing that he must inevitably sink under the fatigues of the journey. He was soon exchanged for three Arab prisoners. They resolved to sell me to Abd-el-Kader, and set out to join him at his camp. I was exposed to every possible kind of ill-usage on the road, blows, threats, insults, and degrading tortures of every kind. To give you one instance among many:—At the camp of one of the tribes on the plain, the Arabs stripped me entirely naked, tied my hands behind my back and fastened me to a tree, whereupon the women and children amused themselves the whole day with flinging stones at me and smearing my face with the most loathsome filth; you can form no idea of my sufferings, the intolerable stench of the filth, the incessant blows inflicted by the stones they threw at me; the children who pinched and bit my thighs all combined to make my torments unbearable.

"After staying some time at Mascara we went to Abd-el-Kader's camp, which was then in the neighbourhood of Tafna. The *Sultan* received me kindly and bought me of my captors. He was very melancholy and completely cast down by his recent defeat by General Bugeaud at Shikak. He had confidently predicted his own victory, founding his prophecy upon a passage of the *Koran*, which foretold the defeat of the Christians during the seventh year of their settlement in Africa.

"Defeat destroyed all his influence; the Arabs forsook their *Sultan* and denied his authority; several of the tribes declared that they would no longer fight under his orders, but would undertake their own defence. They fled in all directions and destroyed everything that lay in their way; they did not even respect Abd-el-Kader's camp, where they cut off and carried away half his tent and pillaged the provisions. It is a great pity that we had no light cavalry at that time, for it would have enabled us to seize Abd-el-Kader's camp.

"Immediately after this defeat, the *Sultan* threw himself into Mascara with fifty horse and a hundred foot, all inhabitants of the town and the sole remnants of his army. A report of a counter-march of General Bugeaud's had spread a panic. Abd-el-Kader's stores were pillaged, and he would never have recovered the blow but for the subsidies of all kinds which he constantly receives from Muley Abd-el-Rachman, emperor of Morocco, without whose assistance he would be utterly unable to support an army.

"When he saw that the Arabs, who but the day before had blindly submitted to his command, were now prepared to shake off his authority, the *Sultan* knew that the prisoners who remained in his camp were doomed to destruction. He resolved to save them, and commanded the thirty negroes who guard his tent to escort M. Lanternier a colonist, his wife a woman of forty, his daughter a lovely girl of fifteen, a German lady of about forty, another of about twenty who was taller and as handsome as Mlle. Lanternier, and myself, as far as Droma, and to protect us from the violence or the insults of the tribes we should pass on our way.

"We started full of gratitude towards Abd-el-Kader, and of confidence in our negro guard, but scarcely had we gone five hundred yards, when the negroes suddenly halted, seized M. Lanternier. and myself, and bound us to a tree with our hands tied behind our backs. The scene which we were then compelled to witness is too hideous to describe; suffice to say, that the four wretched women became the victims of the brutal desires of our negro guard. Even now I often hear in my sleep our imprecations and cries of rage, the howls of the savages, and the sobs of the wretched women. Such is the obedience shown to the commands of the powerful Abd-el-Kader.

"On arriving at Droma, M. Lanternier and I were thrown into a loathsome dungeon, and the four half-dead despairing women into another.

"On the 31st July, Abd-el-Kader sent for me to Mascara, and thence to his camp; his manner towards me was as kind as before, and he again promised me a speedy release by exchange; he also desired me to send for my wife, adding the most solemn protestations, and for a moment the desire of seeing her again almost overcame me, but when I imagined her exposed to blows, threats, and insults, I immediately abandoned the selfish idea of dragging my Clarissa into the misery I was then enduring, and I refused the *Sultan's* offer with many thanks. He then told me his motive for sending for me from Droma, and dictated to me several letters to Algiers and to Oran.

"I have only been in the camp a fortnight, and I am far better off here than in the prisons of Droma, or the tents of the tribes. The *Sultan* puts some restraint upon the hatred of the Arabs towards the Christians, and now your presence will console me under my misfortunes. Besides, you will easily gain the goodwill of Abd-el-Kader, and thus alleviate our hardships, and the governor will be anxious to ransom you, and your deliverance will entail mine. And now good night, if you are cold draw near to me and we shall keep each other warm."

We were awakened very early next morning by the roll of a drum very ill beaten; I instantly rose and spent the whole day in wandering about the camp, and observing the habits and the discipline of Abd-el-Kader's soldiery.

The tents of the infantry are pitched in a circle which encloses those of the cavalry; each tent contains fifteen or twenty men whose horses are tethered outside with ropes lied round their forefeet.

The *Sultan's* tent stands in the very centre of the camp with an open space before it for his horses and those of his attendants: he always has eight or ten horses ready for his own use. A straight avenue is left from the front of his tent to the very edge of the camp where a cannon is placed with its muzzle turned towards the plain. This is the *Sultan's* whole artillery, and in very bad order it is. When I was there it was mounted on a broken French carriage, and the touch-hole was so large that the powder flew out from it in a perfect stream of fire, and burned the hands of the Arabs who fired it. It was only used for salutes and rejoicings. Close to the cannon is the gunner's tent. Behind Abd-el-Kader's tent is that of the muleteers, and round it are picketed the mules which carry the baggage.

Near the kitchen tent are a hundred camels which carry the barley and the biscuits for the soldiers, and a flock of sheep and goats, one of which is given to each tent every Friday. Each tent furnishes two men every night to guard the camp,—one watches from sunset till midnight, the other from midnight till daybreak. During the day there are no guards.

As soon as it dawns the drumbeats and the watch is relieved. A small quantity of detestable biscuit, full of dust and straw, is given to each soldier, and the horsemen give a measure of barley to their horses; they only let them drink once a day at five o'clock, p.m. At four p.m. The soldiers have a meal of boiled barley, and the chiefs of *kuskussu*.

The soldiers have nothing whatever to do, except that from time to time the *aga* of the infantry, following the example of Muftar, endeavours to teach them the drill, in which he was formerly assisted by a German deserter from our Foreign Legion.

The adventures of this German are strange enough. For a year after his desertion he was employed by Abdel-Kader to drill his infantry, but in spite of his zeal and fidelity in the service of his new master, he every day heard the Arabs say that they would shoot him in the first battle, for that they would not submit to be commanded by a Christian hound. The German who did not think proper to await the execution of these threats, took advantage of the peace to go to Oran and present himself to our general. But the general wishing to conciliate Abd-el-Kader, wrote to inform him that he might send for the deserter and do with him as he pleased.

Accordingly some *chaous* were sent to Oran, the deserter was given up to them, and they bound him and dragged him off. On the road they fell in with some French soldiers who were mending it, and the poor fellow began to call out lustily, "Help, my friends! you surely won't let these rascals carry off your comrade who has fought them with you: help! they are going to cut off my head." Hereupon the soldiers threw down their pickaxes, snatched up their muskets, and would certainly have effected a rescue but for a *gendarme* who was sent to protect the *chaous* against any attempt of the kind.

The poor fellow was taken to Mascara where he lay in chains a whole year. In his exasperation at the conduct of the French authorities he turned Mussulman, and was let out of prison; he refused to resume his employment of drill-sergeant, and took to manufacturing gunpowder at Mascara, but finding this trade insufficient for his support he went to Morocco, from whence he hopes to go to Italy.

Since then the *aga* has laboured to teach his ragged and unruly soldiers himself, but with very small success: the little ragamuffins in the streets of Paris go through the exercise far better than Abd-el-Kader's soldiers.

The Arab cavalry now wear a red jacket and Turkish trowsers of the same colour, with a *haick* and a *bernouse* over them, and slippers on their feet; they have a rifle, a sabre, and a dozen cartridges in a box slung over the shoulder with a belt, which never leaves them. Their saddles are made of wood, with a loose cover of morocco leather, and so high before and behind that the rider sits as in a box; the stirrup leathers are very short and the stirrups very large, with sharp points which serve for spurs: they, however, wear spurs besides, which are mere iron spikes about eight or ten inches long.

Only the horses belonging to merchants and destined for long journeys are shod, but none of Abd-el-Kader's. The horsemen put six or eight coarse blankets on their horses' backs to keep the wooden saddle from wounding them. In spite of this precaution, however, nearly all the Arab horses are galled on the back: they are never groomed but merely have some water dashed all over them when they are taken to drink; they are exposed by day and by night to rain, heat, and cold; and accordingly an Arab horse seldom lasts more than six years.

The infantry wear a woollen vest, Turkish trowsers, a black jacket with a hood, and slippers: like the cavalry, they have a rifle, a cartridge box, and a knife at their girdle; the richest among them add to this a dagger, pistols, and a *yataghan*.

In the camp as well as in all other places the Arabs pray six times a day,—at three, six, and eight in the morning, at noon, and at four and eight in the evening: at the hours of devotion the *marabouts* turn to the four cardinal points and call the faithful to prayer with a slow and solemn voice, saying "God is God, and Mahomed is his prophet; come and worship them." A *marabout* then recites the prayer in each tent. The faithful begin by rubbing their hands and faces with dust; they respond to every act of devotion of the *marabout* with an inclination at the words "God is great," and kiss the ground in token of humility; as soon as the prayer is ended they wash their faces.

The band plays three times a day before Abd-el-Kader's tent: three musicians standing, play the hautboy, three others, also standing, beat the tambourine with a stick, and three seated on the ground, play with small sticks upon bowls covered with goatskin. Their *repertoire* is very scanty. I never heard more than three tunes, which they perform till the *Sultan* is tired and dismisses them by a sign.

Each chief has a coffee-maker in his retinue. These coffee-makers erect a tent to which the Arabs go to drink coffee and smoke very bad green tobacco.

CHAPTER 4

French Deserters

Meurice and I were not the only Europeans in the camp, there were three Sardinian prisoners and two French deserters. The latter described to me in the strongest terms the misery they had to endure. In spite of their goodwill and their services the Arabs nearly starved them to death and treated them with the utmost contempt. They bitterly repented having forsaken their flag, and would have been overjoyed to return to it could they have been assured against being shot. One of the deserters, called Jean Mardulin, had rendered all kinds of good offices to Meurice; and indeed the poor fellow well deserved pardon, for the cruel treatment of the Arabs had punished him quite enough for his desertion.

The three Sardinian prisoners appeared more wretched still. I begged one of them to give me an account of the manner in which he and his two companions had fallen into the hands of the Arabs, which he did as follows, after we had stretched ourselves on the ground in the tent.

"Early in July 1836 the three Sardinian coral boats the *St. John Baptist*, the *Conception*, and the *Jesus and Mary*, arrived at a small uninhabited island or rather rock, situated at a few thousand yards from the shore between Cherchell and Mostaganem, near which the owner of the *St. John Baptist* and the *Conception* had discovered a rich bank of coral. We all three served as coral fishers on board these vessels. On arriving at the little island we found two barks, one stranded and the other afloat, the latter was manned by six Moors from Cherchell whom we had formerly known at Algiers.

"We were delighted to fall in with people we knew, and immediately asked the Moors whether we had anything to fear from the Arabs at Ténez. The Moors told us we need fear nothing, as the Arabs had no boats of their own and could not get to the island; they might, indeed, the Moors said, make use of their boats to come and attack us if they found out what we were doing; and in order to prevent any danger of such an event the Moors promised not to leave the island all the time our fishery lasted, on condition that we should supply them with provisions.

"We closed with their offer without hesitation, as we thought we had honest men to deal with, and had often taken a pipe and a cup of coffee with them at Algiers. Accordingly we shared our biscuit and brandy with them and began our fishery, which proved so abundant that in five days we had already got nearly a hundred pounds' worth of coral. We told the Moors how well pleased we were with the success of our fishery, and from that moment their manner was no longer so friendly towards us, and their faces betrayed agitation and disquiet.

"Angelo Floria, the master of the *St. John Baptist*, was the first to remark the change that had taken place in the Moors, whose pro-longed stay on a desert rock had already excited his suspicions. He had long frequented this coast, and knew how much he had to be on his guard against the Arabs: he therefore warned us not to trust our pretended friends too implicitly. Floria's warning made a deep impression on the crews of the three boats, and on the morning of the sixth day we all resolved to leave our anchorage under the island and to withdraw to the westward of the Cape of Ténez, where we knew of a safe anchorage. Unfortunately the wind rose during the day, and the *Conception* and the *Jesus and Mary* were unable to double the cape and forced to return to the island.

"The master of the *St. John Baptist* had reached the anchorage, but when he found that the other two boats did not join him he came back to the island to look for them. Meanwhile, after anchoring the *Conception* and the *Jesus and Mary*, some of us landed on the island, where we were immediately assailed by a shower of balls, and a troop of Arabs, who had been brought by the Moors from Ténez, rushed upon us, brandishing their *yataghans*. Laurentio Figari, the master of the *Jesus and Mary*, was the first who fell by their shot, and his head was instantly cut off with a *yataghan*. My two fellow-prisoners, a little boy, and myself fell into the hands of the Arabs. I received eight wounds from their *yataghans* while endeavouring to revenge myself on the ras-cals who had so basely betrayed us. The rest of the crew jumped into the sea and were shot by the Arabs, who then pillaged and burnt the *Jesus and Mary* and the *Conception*.

"After sharing the plunder, the Arabs set out for Ténez. They halted about half way and deliberated whether they should kill us or not; after a long discussion they determined to take us alive to Abd-el-Kader, in hopes of getting some more money from him.

"We stopped two days at Ténez, where the generous kindness of the inhabitants made up for the sufferings and privations of our journey. The *kait* of Ténez visited us continually, and asked us numberless questions about the coral fishery: our account of it amused him very much, and he took great interest in our fate, and prevented the Arabs from beating us. I shall never forget the kindness of the women of Ténez, who never left me the whole time I was there, nor ceased from rubbing my wounds with butter and honey; they also gave us white bread and fruit, and overwhelmed the poor little boy with caresses. I could hardly believe that I was not at Genoa, instead of in a heathen country, so great was their charity.

"We left Ténez on the third day and soon arrived at Abd-el-Kader's camp, where we have been prisoners for a month. We do not know whether we shall be ransomed or exchanged, and we suffer continual misery and ill-usage, notwithstanding which my wounds are quite healed, and we all three hope that, with the assistance of the Blessed Virgin and the French governor, we shall in the end recover our freedom and return home.

"Abd-el-Kader sent the little boy to his wife, who is just as kind to him as the Arabs are cruel to us men. The Arab women will soon coax the poor child into forgetting the Blessed Virgin, his own country, and his mother, and they will teach him their prayers and make a Mahomedan of him. We have not seen him since we came here, but, perhaps, when Abd-el-Kader shifts his camp we may meet him somewhere.

"I hope, Sir, that when you write to the generals at Oran or Algiers you will not forget to say a word in favour of us three poor Christians."

I assured them that I would say as much for them as for myself, whereupon they took their leave.

I had already asked the *Sultan's* permission to write to Algiers and Oran, to acquaint the authorities with my captivity, and my arrival at Abd-el-Kader's camp. At eight o'clock that evening I was conducted to his tent, where he gave me his own pen, made of a reed, a bit of coarse paper about the size of my hand, and his inkstand, which was made of brass, of an oblong shape, with an inkbottle at one end and a drawer for the pens at the other. A slave brought a brass candlestick, such as stand on the altar of a village church in France. I lay on the ground, and with the *Sultan's* jewel-box for a table, I wrote one letter to Admiral Dufresne, and another to General Rapatel, describing the sufferings of Abd-el-Kader's captives, and entreating them to negotiate our exchange as quickly as possible. I then delivered the two letters to Abd-el-Kader, who promised to forward them next day.

We were awakened very early in the morning by the chief of our tent shouting, "Dogs of Christians, sons of dogs, got up! the tent is coming down, for the *Sultan* has ordered the camp to be raised." Scarce were the words out of his mouth than the whole tent came tumbling down upon Meurice and myself. This was one of the thousand pleasantries with which the Arabs continually entertained us. We were still struggling to disentangle ourselves from the tent, in which we lay caught like fish in a net, when a drum beat the *reveille*, which was followed in a few minutes by the signal of march for the infantry, which accordingly started.

The camels, mules, and pack horses were immediately loaded with all the camp equipage, stowed in panniers woven of the leaves of the dwarf palm. A third beat of the drum gave the signal of departure to the muleteers and camel drivers. Meurice and I were placed in the centre of this detachment, which was under the command of Ben Faka. In obedience to the *Sultan's* order, we were mounted on the two mules which carry Abd-el-Kader's own coffers; the Italian sailors were worse off,—they rode on camels. Among the baggage I observed eight very ill-joined chests; these contained the reserve cartridges.

Whenever the camp is raised Abd-el-Kader, who, like every other Arab, begins his prayers at three in the morning, does not cease from them until all the other tents are struck, and it is time for the slaves to strike his, he then quits it, and seats himself at a short distance on a silken cushion surrounded by the *marabouts* and chiefs. Meanwhile the horsemen assemble, and place themselves in a line on his right hand, with Muftar at their head, and the thirty negro slaves are drawn up in a line on las left. The chiefs and the *marabouts* next mount their horses, and as soon as the baggage has passed the limits of what was the camp, a slave comes forward leading the Sultan's horse, followed by another bearing the footstool which he uses as a horse-block.

Abd-el-Kader's favourite horse is a magnificent black charger; he is the best rider I ever saw among the Arabs; and as his legs are disproportionately short for the length of his body, the Arab fashion of short stirrups, by concealing this defect, sets off his figure to great advantage, and his appearance on horseback is at once graceful and imposing. As soon as the *Sultan* is mounted, the chiefs give the signal of departure; the nine musicians ride at the head of the column, followed by eight Arabs bearing long rifles in red cloth cases; I have often asked leave to examine them, but the Arabs always answered, "They are the arms of the *Sultan*; a dog of a Christian like thee is not worthy to behold them." Next come four more horsemen bearing the four flags which I have already described, and then Abd-el- Kader, in the centre of a line of horsemen: behind him are the thirty negroes, and they are followed by all the rest of the cavalry pell-mell. The Arabs never set out on an expedition until the sun has risen.

No order or discipline is kept on their marches; thus, if a soldier sees a fruit tree or a solitary tent he leaves the line to strip the one or pillage the other.

Two strangely-harnessed mules, more lean and broken-winded than hackney coach horses, drag the solitary cannon. Not a day passes on which it is not overturned and half buried in the mud. I hope, for the sake of the poor gunners, that it will at last be left behind fast stuck, which will save them a vast deal of useless trouble and burning of their fingers.

We left El Kaala on the 17th of August, and reached the plain of Mostaganem at one o'clock the same day, where we encamped, at a distance of four leagues from the town. The Arabs always turn their tents with the opening towards the east, and such accuracy do they acquire by habit, that at whatever time they pitch their tents they are invariably greeted by the first rays of the rising sun. Ben Faka determines the situation of the camp, and superintends in person the erection of the *Sultan's* tent and the watering of the ground all about it. These arrangements are scarcely completed when the screeching of the music announces the approach of Abd-el-Kader.

A number of horsemen detach themselves from the main body, which they precede by about ten minutes, and gallop to the camp, where they suddenly wheel round, and return at full speed to meet the advancing column, aiming their rifles full at the *Sultan* all the while. When they are within shot of him they turn their guns a little aside, and send their bullets whistling about his ears.

This salute goes on till he is within the camp, when the horsemen range themselves in a line on the right of the tent, and the thirty negroes on the left, the band plays as loud as ever it can, and the cannon announces the arrival of Abd-el-Kader to the neighbouring tribes: the

Sultan makes his horse prance along the line formed by his cavalry, and glances proudly around him, two slaves open the curtains of the tent, the horse rears and neighs violently as he enters it and tramples upon the carpet, while the Arabs stand in open-mouthed admiration of the grace and activity of their *Sultan*; the faithful Ben Faka offers his back to assist his lord in dismounting, and a slave leads away the horse and walks him up and down before the tent for ten minutes; the *marabouts* and chiefs surround Abd-el-Kader, who orders the drums to beat, upon which the ranks are broken and men and horses repair to the tents, which the baggage attendants have already pitched for them.

The chiefs of the neighbouring tribes on hearing the sound of the cannon hasten to pay their respects to the *Sultan*; they crowd pell-mell into his tent, rush upon Abd-el-Kader, who is seated on his sofa, and kiss his hand, the hood formed by the folds of his *haick*, and the skirts of his *bernouse*; in return he makes the motion of kissing their hands.

On this occasion very few of the neighbouring Arabs came to salute him, as most of them were allied with the French; and in the evening only a little *kuskussu* was brought to feed his troops.

In the middle of the night the drums beat a *reveille*, everybody jumped up, and the report was spread that Ibrahim, *Bey* of Mostaganem, had made a sortie with his troops, and was about to attack Abd-el-Kader. The *Sultan* left the camp at the head of all his cavalry to reconnoitre the movements of the *Bey*. I lay down behind a package, very indifferent to all the confusion and excitement which prevailed in the camp, and slept soundly while poor Meurice vainly sought for me in all directions, and at last, fancying I had made my escape, was in perfect despair, and wandered about mentally accusing me of unkindness, until I awoke and put an end to his distress.

Abd-el-Kader returned to the camp at daybreak, without having fallen in with Ibrahim, and brought back the news that the French troops had left Oran four days before. As he was by no means reassured as to the *Bey's* movements, he ordered the camp to be raised, and by eleven o'clock the same morning we were back again within five minutes' walk of El-Kaala.

The inhabitants of the town, whose resources were already exhausted by the support of his troops, were so ill-pleased at the *Sultan's* return that none of them came to pay their respects to him, and the Turks living in the town fled into the mountains carrying with them all their money. As soon as the *Sultan* became aware of their disaffection, he repaired to Kaala with fifty horsemen, and soon returned with a cargo of carpets and other articles which had been taken by main force from the most refractory of the citizens, who now fired a salute to testify the joy they felt at the *Sultan's* presence, while their goods were being distributed before Abd-el-Kader's tent.

CHAPTER 5

The Beautiful Black Slave Girl

On the 23rd of August, at five in the morning, we again left Kaala, and marched northward; after a march of seven hours, we encamped on the very edge of the plain of Mostaganem, near the River Scheliff. Our camp stood in a grove of ilexes and gum trees on the top of a mountain, commanding the plain; just such a spot as was selected by knights of old to build their castles on, for the better convenience of robbing travellers, oppressing their serfs, and defending themselves against their neighbours.

Abd-el-Kader's tent was pitched near a fresh and abundant spring, and the weather being oppressively hot, Zaka, the *Sultan's* cup-bearer, ordered the slaves to dig two little channels to convey the water to the tent, where it was received into trenches immediately under the hangings, which were raised just enough to admit a current of air cooled by the water which surrounded the tent, and gave it the appearance of an island.

I am too poor a hand at my pen, to attempt a description of the beautiful and fertile plain which lay at our feet covered with crops of various kinds, fruit trees, herds, flocks and tents. In spite of my position I could not help sharing the general satisfaction inspired by this delightful scene which promised such plentiful supplies to the troops. Abd-el-Kader, in a fit of generosity and good humour, sent me twelve pieces of eight *moussounés* each, (almost four shillings.) which I was to share with Meurice. This munificent and public manifestation of goodwill raised my spirits, and filled me with the hope of a speedy deliverance, which was strengthened by the knowledge that the Arabs, whom General Bugeaud had carried as prisoners to Marseilles, were as impatient as myself to be restored to freedom and to their country.

In the morning a supply of melons, peaches, figs, and grapes arrived at the camp, and we feasted on what fell to our share; the grapes were better than the very best in France. I spent a few hours in wandering about and admiring the beauty of the scenery, and then stretched myself in the shade and indulged in a reverie, out of which I was awakened at about four in the afternoon by the arrival of all the surrounding tribes, who came to bring their subsidies. Each tribe was preceded by its *kait*, on horseback and armed only with a stick, then came all the tribe—men, women, and children, two and two, bearing on their heads dishes filled with *kuskussu*; the richest Arabs walked apart from the line carrying whole sheep, spitted and roasted on a stake.

When they had reached Abd-el-Kader's tent, the chief of each tribe stepped forward and informed him that they had brought the tribute, the Arabs set their dishes on the ground before the tent and thrust the points of the spits on which the sheep were impaled into the ground. These dishes of *kuskussu* crowned, some with honey, some with hard eggs, some with raisins, others with boiled fowls or quarters of mutton, wore a most varied and tempting appearance. The Arabs then rushed into the tent to present their respects to the *Sultan*, while several of them took advantage of the confusion to steal the viands spread upon the earth, and it was only by the most vigorous application of their sticks that the *kaits* could succeed in maintaining tolerable order. Abd-el-Kader then cast a glance upon the dishes disposed before his tent, and Ben Faka distributed them among the troops.

When the *Sultan* had finished his repast, Ben Faka, who always serves it, brought the remains to our tent. A piece of leather was spread in the centre of the carpet, and a dish of *kuskussu* which had been begun by the *Sultan* was placed upon it. Ben Faka and several *marabouts* squatted in a circle round the leathern tablecloth, and began to devour the *kuskussu* and a sheep which we had for supper, without any bread, tearing the mutton with their fingers, and throwing the bones and scraps back into the dish, as the *Sultan* had done before them, when they had eaten their fill, the dish passed into third hands, and formed the supper of Abd-el-Kader's slaves, who gnawed the bones and scraps of meat like so many dogs.

During this last stage of the repast Ben Faka called Meurice and me and threw us a piece of meat, which we ate in the Arab fashion with our fingers and without bread: he also bestowed upon us a handful or so of *kuskussu*. The water was brought in goatskins, and all the guests drank out of the same bowl which was never washed. I need not add that the prisoners were always served last. In spite of all this we thought our dinner excellent, and in order worthily to conclude a repast in which we had eaten meat, I asked Ben Faka's leave to have coffee brought to us.

"Coffee for a Christian hound!" said he; "and who is to pay for it?"

"Did not the *Sultan* give me six pieces (two shillings), this morning?" replied I; "and shall I not whenever I am exchanged proclaim his munificence to my fellow-countrymen?"

These words softened the hard heart of Ben Faka, and he ordered his coffee-maker to bring us some coffee. He then began to boast to us of the power and the wealth of his master and of his own influence with him, and exhibited, with the greatest pride, a snuff-box with a little mirror in the lid,—a treasure which excited indescribable envy and admiration among all the Arabs who were present. We soon perceived that the drift of his conversation was to induce us to solicit his protection and to offer him presents, and poor Meurice, who was always on the watch for an opportunity of conciliating his tormentors, immediately promised to send him a gold snuff-box from Algiers as soon as he was set free. The delight of this Arab minister of finance, and his promises of kindness to the dog of a Christian, may easily be conceived.

The slave of Ben Faka's coffee-maker interrupted our conversation by bringing the coffee in two little earthenware cups on a tin tray: the cups have no handles, but are fixed in small brass saucers; the coffee seemed to me delicious—it was served with the grounds; and the two cups sweetened with brown sugar, and a couple of pipes to smoke, cost a penny.

Even now I cannot think of that day without emotion: it was so unlike all the rest of my captivity; we suffered neither ill usage, cold, nor hunger; the weather was beautiful, we had plenty of fruits, and Abd-el-Kader and Ben Faka were even kind to us: in short, to us it was a day of positive enjoyment.

It has been asserted that Abd-el-Kader received no supplies from Morocco; this statement is contradicted by facts which I myself witnessed. On the 7th of August, 1836, a convoy arrived at the *Sultan's* camp, from Morocco, bringing flints, scull-caps, slippers, trowsers, and cloaks enough for six hundred men. On the 10th of August there came fifteen camels loaded with powder and ball, also from Morocco. On the 25th of August Abd-el-Kader received from Morocco a store of biscuits and saltpetre. Every time that these supplies arrived at the camp the Arabs testified the greatest joy and exultation, and received the chief of the convoy with the same honours that they pay to Abd-el-Kader.

On the 28th of August two Arab spies came to the camp, one of them bringing a number of gun-flints which he had bought at Oran, and the other some despatches entrusted to him by the French authorities at Tlemsen for the commandant at Oran, and to which he was to take back an answer.

Abd-el-Kader unsealed them, and having sent for Meurice, ordered him to read them. Meurice obeyed, and the *Sultan* resealed and sent them on to their address.

A few days after, the same Arab filling the double office of courier to the French and spy to Abd-el-Kader, returned to the camp with the answer from General Létang the commandant of Oran, to the commandant of Tlemsen. Abd-el-Kader sent for me, and after very carefully unsealing General Létang's letters, he ordered me to read them aloud. In them the general informed the commandant of Tlemsen, that he had returned from his expedition against the Beni Amers, having achieved it without striking a single blow, and that he had plundered the silos[1] of the Arabs.

The officers of the brig *Loiret*, added General Létang, were foolish enough to go out shooting at Arzew, and Lieutenant de France fell into the hands of the Arabs.

I took very good care not to read the first part of the letter, but only what related to myself.

"Is that all?" said the *Sultan*; "surely thou hast deceived me?"

"Read it yourself," said I, "and you will see." I was certain he could not read French, although he speaks it pretty well. I was then dismissed, and on returning to the tent I informed Meurice of what had just happened; and it was fortunate for me that I did so, for scarce had I finished my story when a *marabout* came in and summoned him to appear before the *Sultan*, and had he read what I had passed over, no doubt the *chaous* would soon have disabled me from ever telling that Abd-el-Kader opens the despatches of our generals.

On the 29th of August the camp was again broken up, and after a march of six hours we halted on the banks of the Ouet Mina, a nar-

---

1. The Arab subterranean granaries and barns, which are carefully covered with lime, and excavated with so much art as to exclude all moisture, and preserve the contents for years; the only access to them is through a funnel-shaped hole at the top, barely large enough to admit a man.

row but very rapid stream which rises to the east of Tekedemta and falls into the Schellif at about six leagues from the coast. The Schellif, which is the principal river of the country, rises among the mountains to the south of Milianah, runs from east to west, and falls into the sea near Cape Ivi, between the Cape of Ténez and the Gulf of Arzew.

Ben Faka placed the camp on a hill adjoining the chain of mountains which overlooks the western part of the plain of Milianah. The site was as beautiful as the one we had just left: not far from our tent was a lofty cascade, the waters of which fell into the plain below, where they soon disappeared. If they were received in a basin and thence carried in small channels over the plain, the parched earth would soon be changed into green meadows which would afford far better food for the cows and horses of the Arabs than the weeds and briars which they are now forced to eat; and the harvests of wheat and barley would be very abundant; for though the Arab plough only scratches the very surface of the earth. I have seen one grain of wheat produce six or eight stalks. This province generally has very few trees, but the mountains which surround it are covered with ilexes and gum trees.

Abd-el-Kader laid a double tax upon the surrounding tribes to punish them for having given a favourable reception to Ibrahim, *Bey* of Mostaganem. Every day the horsemen brought to the camp great booty in horses, sheep, and oxen; and in Abd-el-Kader's tent the whole day was passed in counting the money which had been seized: this does not imply that the sums were immense, but that the Arabs count over their money ten or fifteen times. The chief secretary, whom by virtue of his office I am bound to consider as the most enlightened man in the camp, used frequently to come into our tent, and crouching behind a bale of goods, entirely hidden under his *haick*, count and recount his money for hours together.

In spite of the most stringent measures and of the zeal displayed by the *kaits* in collecting the tribute, it was hard to make the Arabs pay it, and Abd-el-Kader sent a party of horsemen to their tents, who returned in the evening laden with every kind of booty, and driving before them herds of horses, cattle, sheep, women, children, and negroes.

At the news of the arrival of these prisoners a number of Arabs came to the camp, in order to see whether they might not be able to buy a few negroes, or a woman or so, a bargain. If, after casting a rapid glance over the slaves who were crouching on the ground, the buyer saw one whose appearance struck his fancy, he made him rise and examined all his limbs, as we examine a horse or a bull, made him open his mouth, and, if it was a woman, pressed her breasts to see whether there was milk in them. The unfortunate wretches bore it all with the most perfect indifference, and when the bargain was struck, they followed their new masters with an air of utter insensibility.

Among the prisoners for sale who were in our tent, was a beautiful black girl of about fourteen; she had large soft black eyes, lips like coral, and teeth like the pearls set in the handle of a *yataghan*; her legs were like those of a race horse, and her feet and hands smaller than those of a Spanish woman; her shape was perfect, and the slenderness of her waist contrasted beautifully with the fullness of her hips; for the poor girl, contrary to the custom of the women of this country, had confined her white *haick* round her middle with a red worsted cord. Her beauty and the fineness and cleanliness of her dress clearly showed that she had been the property of wealthy people. The poor girl laid herself on the ground beside me, weeping and lamenting, and refused the food that was offered to her.

Seeing her so beautiful and so unhappy, I tried to comfort her; but she said, "I was so happy in the tent from which they robbed me, and now I shall be made to sleep outside with the horses: I shall have no *kuskussu* to eat, and I shall wear a torn and dirty *haick*;" and she wept again.

Before long, a chief of the Garrabas came into the tent: he had brought the head of a French soldier whom he had surprised that morning in a field near Mostaganem, so that he was welcome in the camp. He was rich and wanted to buy slaves. At the sight of the young negress his eyes brightened with pleasure, and he ordered her to rise. The slave obeyed, she was subjected to the most minute examination and found faultless. The Garraba turned to Ben Faka, and said, "Fifty *boutjous?*"

"I must have eighty *boutjous* (10/.) for her," said Ben Faka.

"She is not worth them."

"Did'st thou ever see so beautiful a negress?—Open thy mouth."

The slave obeyed.

"Look, what teeth! there is not one missing!—Walk."

Th slave walked.

"What hips! what a firm and graceful step! She is a virgin too.—Open thy *haick* and thy shift."

The slave did as she was commanded.

"Press her breasts; she has no more milk than a newborn lamb. Don't weep slave, or the *chaous* shall dry thy tears with his stick."

The girl wiped her eyes.

"Eighty *boutjous*."

"Sixty. She is not strong; she will not be able to carry the dung out of the stable."

"In two years she will carry the dung of all the horses belonging to thy tent. Eighty *boutjous*."

"Seventy."

"Her hands are delicate; she has never worked. Eighty *boutjous*. Yea or nay? the *Sultan* waits for me."

The Garraba paid them and bade his slave follow him; the poor girl left the tent fixing on me her eyes bathed in tears. I saw the Garraba stop at the *Sultan's* tent to receive the price of the Frenchman's head, and in a few minutes they left the camp, and I lost sight of the poor black girl.

CHAPTER 6

Horrible Execution of a Prisoner

On the 2nd of September the courier from Tlemsen brought several letters which Abd-el-Kader opened, read, sealed, and sent to their destination.

The energetic measures taken by Abd-el-Kader against the neighbouring tribes had failed in reducing them to complete submission; they only waited for an opportunity to shake off his authority. One of Abd-el-Kader's uncles, a *marabout*, declared himself independent of the *Sultan*, and refused to pay the tribute: he was immediately joined by the Beni-Flitas and Houledscherifs, two numerous, rich, and powerful tribes which inhabit a part of the country watered by the Ouet Mina and the adjoining mountains. They refused any longer to acknowledge Abd-el-Kader as their *Sultan*, and submitted to the authority of his uncle.

The *Sultan* again sent a party of horsemen to claim the tribute from his uncle, who instead of paying it, sent the following answer:—

"Thou wert nothing before the coming of the French; thou wert nothing until thou hadst made a peace with those unbelievers. I was greater and holier than thou; and it was in the hope of usurping my authority, O Abd-el-Kader, that thou madest a treaty with the Christians; to them thou owest thy greatness and thy power. When thou thoughtest thyself great enough, thou brakest the treaty with the French, and now thou wilt that we should acknowledge thee as our *Sultan*. But I have ever been greater and holier than thou, and never will I bow before thee. Neither will I pay the tribute which thy horsemen demand in thy name."

This letter, of which I remember only the most striking passages, threw Abd-el-Kader into a state of melancholy and indecision which lasted several days, and spread general consternation in the camp. The

Arabs saw with horror that they would perhaps be compelled to turn their weapons against their brethren, and they felt that a civil war among themselves would secure forever the dominion of the French.

Abd-el-Kader sent courier upon courier to his uncle to persuade him to submission, but the *marabout* was deaf to all his arguments, and always returned the same answer—"I have ever been greater and holier than thou, Abd-el-Kader, and never will I acknowledge thee as my *Sultan*. Send no more horsemen unto me for I will not pay tribute to thee." While these negotiations were going on, Abd-el-Kader called together all the tribes on the banks of the Ouet Mina and the Schellif, but they were unwilling to involve themselves in hostilities with their neighbours. Scarce a hundred horsemen answered the summons, and these nearly all took flight after the first day: those who remained were watched and kept within the camp.

Desertion Had already begun among the *Sultan's* regular troops, and a spirit of bitter discontent and depression reigned throughout the camp. Several of the tribes, when threatened by Abd-el-Kader, replied that they knew the way to Mostaganem, and that if he molested them they would go and place themselves under the protection of the French.

Hereupon Abd-el-Kader seized the principal chiefs: four of them were kept in the camp with their feet in irons; four others, chained together by the neck, were thrown into prison at Mascara.

On the 8th of September a troop of horsemen brought nine Jews whom they had seized in the environs of Mostaganem, and the heads of three Turks whom they had killed. The Jews had been cruelly treated by the Arabs; they were chained together by the throat, their feet were torn and bruised, and their bodies covered with wounds. When they were brought before the *Sultan* they resorted to a lie, (if indeed it be a lie to deceive an enemy in order to save one's life.) and said that when the French took Mostaganem they had fled to Mascara with their families and their possessions, that the French had forced them to return to Mostaganem, and that they were again trying to escape to Mascara when the horsemen seized them. The *Sultan* upon hearing this bade them send for their property and their families, and return to Mascara; adding, that if they obeyed, no harm should befall them, but if not, that their heads should keep company with those of the three Turks.

"Abd-el-Kader is great, powerful, and holy," said the poor Jews; "and we will go and dwell in Mascara with our wives, our children, and our goods."

The three Turks' heads and that of the French soldier which the Garraba had brought, were exhibited in front of the *Sultan's* tent for two days; on the third the children had them to play with, after which they were thrown outside the camp to the birds of prey.

On the morning of the 10th of September Abd-el-Kader started, with all his forces and the solitary cannon, to attack the Flitas and Houledscherifs, leaving one man to each tent to guard the camp. The insurgent tribes, who were prepared for an attack, had already sent their women, children, and cattle up into the mountains, and the *Sultan* found them drawn up in order of battle on the high mountain which skirts the plain of Milianah, at the *marabout* nearest to the Ouet Mina and the Schellif. The fight lasted the whole day, and the cannon was fired seven or eight times, loaded with stones in default of balls.

In the evening Abd-el-Kader returned to the camp, bringing back twelve dead and eight wounded. I never could obtain any precise account of the result of the battle, but the dejection of the *Sultan* and his troops plainly showed that they had not been victorious. The horsemen brought back five heads and drove before them a troop of women and children who had not been able to reach the mountains: the unfortunate creatures were all thrown into the prisons of Mascara. One man had been taken alive: he was brought before the *Sultan* as soon as the latter had dismounted.

"Thou wert taken among the rebels?"

"I was."

"What hast thou to say in thy defence?"

"I was compelled to fight against thee."

"Thou shouldest then have fled to my camp."

"But"—

"Enough."

Abd-el-Kader raised his hand, and the unhappy man was dragged away by the *chaous*. One of the *chaous* had lost his son in the battle, and had seen his head hanging to the saddle-bow of a Beni-Flita: with tears and lamentations he now implored the other *chaous* to grant him the favour of putting the prisoner to death with his own unaided hand. He at last obtained it, and immediately rushed upon the Beni-Flita, and cut off his hands and feet with his *yataghan*. The children shouted for joy at this horrid sight, and the revengeful father watched with delight the hideous contortions of the victim who rolled in the dust at his feet, shrieking with rage and pain, and imploring his tormenter to cut off his head.

When the Beni-Flita at length fainted from loss of blood, the *chaous* passed a rope round his middle, and dragged him by it outside the enclosure of the camp; the children brought together a quantity of brushwood and dry brandies, and set fire to them, and on this pile the *chaous* threw the still living Beni-Flita.

It was night, and the flames threw a lurid glare upon the dark tents: the piercing shrieks of the Beni-Flita long sounded through the camp. I covered my head with my *haick*, and groaned when I thought that only a few leagues from this savage camp were the outposts of a noble and generous nation.

Within a few days of my arrival at Abd-el-Kader's camp I was covered with the lice with which the Arabs are infested The *Sultan* himself in the midst of the most serious discussion picks them off his *haick*, rolls them gravely between his finger and thumb, and throws them upon the carpet. These vermin are of a monstrous size, white with a black stripe along the back, which swells with the blood they suck from their unhappy victims. Fortunately for us, they did not much frequent our hair and beards, but they laid their eggs in the seams of our clothes, and were hatched upon us in myriads. The Arabs are so used to them that they treated us with the greatest scorn when they saw our efforts to rid ourselves of these tormenters.

One day we asked Abd-el-Kader to allow us to bathe in the Ouet Mina, in order to wash off the vermin and the dust with which our bodies were covered. The *Sultan* granted our request, and sent one of his negroes to protect us against the Arabs. I cannot describe the pleasure of stretching our weary and heated limbs in the clear cool water; but in two days the dust and the lice were as bad as ever. We slept on the bare ground, and as the nights were intensely cold we crept close to each other, but as soon as the blood began to circulate at all in our benumbed bodies the lice resumed their attacks, and we again sought the cold to escape from their intolerable pricking.

On the day after the battle, the 11th of September, the camp was raised at daybreak, and from sunrise till three o'clock, p.m., we marched towards the south-east along horrible roads, over mountains covered with gum trees, beeches, junipers, and ilexes.

Ben Faka pitched the camp on a fine *plateau*, from whence we could see the traces of the habitations of the Beni-Flitas, who had joined Abd-el-Kader's uncle. As soon as the usual salute had been fired, the horsemen, without even giving their horses time to breathe, started in all directions, to plunder the silos of the Beni-Flitas. They soon returned laden with wheat, barley, and straw, but no roast mutton or *kuskussu* was brought that evening.

When Abd-el-Kader found that all the inhabitants of the district had left it and joined the refractory *marabout* in the mountains, and that he was in danger of wanting provisions, he determined to move the camp again, and accordingly we marched for some days through a perfectly deserted country.

At length, on the 17th of September, after a southward march of eight hours, we came to an inhabited district. A few tribes brought some horses and a little money to the *Sultan*, but these supplies were few and scanty. An Arab came from Mascara with the news that General Létang had left Oran, and that the Garrabas had taken a great number of cattle and sheep from the Douairs. The loss sustained by the Douairs caused great rejoicing in our camp, and the horsemen galloped about firing their rifles in honour of the victorious Garrabas.

On the 19th of September the tents were again struck, and after five hours' march Ben Faka halted on the slope of a mountain just below a *marabout* which was flanked by a tower at each corner. The surrounding country was well peopled, and the fields covered with wheat and barley. From the heights above us, one could see the tents of the tribes dotted about the plain and the slope of the mountain.

At about six hours' march from this place are the ruins of the ancient city of Tekedemta, which Abd-el-Kader had long wished to rebuild; and, with the view of obtaining from the neighbouring tribes provisions and assistance of all kinds towards this undertaking, he now remitted to them the payment of tribute, at the same time telling the *kaits* that he should expect to receive at Tekedemta all that they would otherwise have brought to him now.

Next day, the 20th of September, we left the *marabout* with the four towers and marched to the neighbourhood of Tekedemta. While the troops were employed in preparing the tents, Abd-el-Kader mounted a fresh horse, and went to visit the ruins, accompanied by a few *marabouts*.

We were now in the midst of high mountains covered with gum trees, beeches, ilexes, and junipers, which by their size and number clearly proved that it was very long since the Arabs inhabited this country; for they soon destroy all the trees within their reach, partly by the quantity of wood which they use both for cooking and for the bonfires which they burn all night to keep off the wild beasts and to warm the sentinels, and partly by their custom of clearing a path through the forest by setting fire to the trees as they stand.

Several Moors from Mascara arrived on the same day as ourselves, with fifty asses carrying baskets, pickaxes, shovels, and all kinds of implements for building, and as soon as the *Sultan* returned to the camp, he dispatched all the muleteers and some of his negroes to clear the ground on which the ancient Casabah of Tekedemta had stood. On the following day he sent a number of soldiers to go on with the clearing and to build a redoubt.

All these workmen were unpaid, and ill-will and discontent soon appeared among them, they went grumbling to their work, and the *Sultan* was forced to superintend them in person, or nothing was done.

On the 26th an Arab courier brought Abd-el-Kader a letter from the prisoners who had been taken at Trara-Sickak by General Bugeaud and conveyed to France. The contents of the letter produced a great sensation, and joy was painted on every face. The *Sultan* sent for me, and said, "I have received a letter from my Arabs at Marseilles; the Christians treat them kindly."

"How then," said I, "can a *Sultan* so great and holy as thou suffer us to be treated so ill? The nights are cold among these mountains, and whilst thy Arabs at Marseilles sleep on good mattresses, wrapped in warm blankets, we have not even a rug to lie upon at night."

Abd-el-Kader smiled graciously, and sent for Ben Faka, whom he commanded to give us whatever we asked for, and first of all a rug to sleep on at night.

CHAPTER 7

Attempt to Convert Me

On the morning of the 29th I begged the *Sultan* to allow Meurice and myself to go and see the ruins of Tekedemta, and the works carried on there by his troops. He told us to go without fear, and ordered one of his negroes to accompany us. We accordingly started, and after walking for half an hour we reached the ruins of Tekedemta. The ground on which the city stood is very broken and without a trace of vegetation; part of the wall of a fort was still standing, it was about ten feet thick at the base, and a few feet from the ground it fell back to the thickness of about seven feet. The wall was defended by nine towers, the foundations of which were still to be seen: they were without the line of the wall, but joined to it.

The whole enclosure is one thousand eight hundred feet long, by one thousand one hundred and fifty feet broad. The remains within the fort prove that it was filled with streets, shops, and houses. On a hill a few hundred yards from the citadel, may be traced the foundation of the ancient Casabah or *Bey's* palace, surrounded by fortifications: on these foundations Abd-el-Kader is going to build a new one. At the foot of the hill, about ten minutes' walk from these ruins, flows the Ouet Mina. The site of the town is commanded by lofty mountains on every side, except towards the west, where a gentle ascent leads up to it. A road runs from hence to Mascara.

After examining the ruins, we went towards a redoubt which Abd-el-Kader was constructing at a distance of two hundred yards to the eastward of the Casabah, and there we found the *Sultan* with his chief secretary, Ben Abu, and Milud-Ben-Arrach, reclining on the earth, which had been thrown up in digging a ditch. There was nothing in his costume to distinguish him from the common labourers: he wore a huge hat plaited of the leaves of the dwarf palm tree, with brims full three feet in circumference fastened with a worsted cord and tassels to the crown, which was at least a foot and a half high and pointed at the top.

He greeted us kindly, and motioned us to sit beside him: encouraged by this gracious reception I ventured to ask him what were his projects in rebuilding Tekedemta.

"My predecessors, who dwelt in this city," replied he, "ruled from Tunis to Morocco, and I will restore it to its ancient splendour; I will gather together the tribes in this place, where we shall be secure from the attacks of the French, and when all my forces are collected I will descend from this steep rock like a vulture from his nest, and drive the Christians out of Algiers, Oran and Bona: if, indeed, you were content with those three cities I would suffer you to remain there, for the sea is not mine and I have no ships; but you want our plains and our inland cities and our mountains; nay, you even covet our horses, our tents, our camels, and our women, and you leave your own country to come and take that in which Mahomed has placed his people. But your *Sultan* is not a saint and a horseman as I am, and your horses will stumble and fall on our mountains, for they are not sure-footed like our horses, and your soldiers will die of sickness, and those whom the pestilence has spared will fall by the bullets of the Arab horsemen, for you are dogs who never pray to God."

I made no reply to this pompous harangue, but went to look at the works. The men were digging a ditch to enclose an area of about fifty square yards: they carried the earth which they dug out towards the spot on which the redoubt was to stand, as we do in throwing up blockhouses. This fort was intended to receive a garrison for the protection of the workmen. It stands on a slope and is commanded by the ruins of the ancient citadel and by a hill, so that even without cannon the garrison might easily be forced to evacuate.

After taking a cursory view of these works, we returned to the ruins of the citadel, still accompanied by the negro, who could not understand what pleasure we could find in walking about among old stones, and who kept muttering that we were "dogs" and "asses" all the time that we were exploring.

At sunset we returned to the camp, where we heard a great uproar, and soon discovered a crowd of Arabs fighting and struggling in the midst of a dense cloud of dust: they were all rolling on the ground and wrestling together, screaming, swearing, and abusing each other, while the *chaous* were showering blows to the right and to the left upon them.

We hastened to our tent somewhat alarmed at the scuffle, and on asking the cause of it, we heard that the *chaous* had been distributing barley among the horsemen, and that a few measures had been left over: the Arabs instantly rushed upon them, and in their efforts to seize a few handfuls of barley they made the riot we had seen.

I was sitting in the tent waiting for supper, when one of Abd-el-Kader's cousins, a *marabout*, hastily entered. "I am sent by the *Sultan*," said he, "to ask whether thou wilt embrace the true faith and remain among us, and to tell thee that if thou wilt, he will make thee as powerful as himself."

I replied, that I wished to return to my own people.

"Thou shalt have women, horses, arms, and plenty of powder, and thou shalt be as rich, as great, and as powerful as the *Sultan* himself."

"If," said I, "the *Sultan* will give me the command of a ship I will become a Mahomedan, and I will go to the coast of Cherchell to fish for coral with the Italian prisoners, and we will enrich the *Sultan*."

I suppose the *marabout* guessed where I should really go if my conditions were accepted, for he left the tent without saying another word.

While we were at the ruins, the tribes who dwelt at half a day's march from Tekedemta had brought *kuskussu* and a roasted sheep, and the people of Milianah, all kinds of fruit. Ben Faka regaled us sumptuously with white bread, fruit, and a roast leg of mutton. The white loaves were brought to the camp every day by the tribes, and were the only pay given to Abd-el-Kader's workmen.

Just as I was ending my splendid repast, Ben Faka came to me with Abd-el-Kader's command to go his tent. I hastened to obey the summons, full of the hope of liberty. The *Sultan* received me as usual, with enquiries after my health, after which he commanded me to write to General Rapatel, and to ask him whether he would give in exchange for me three of the Arab prisoners at Marseilles, to be selected by Abd-el-Kader. I refused to write unless the *Sultan* would at the same time name a ransom for my fellow-prisoners, and for Lanternier and the four women at Droma.

After a very long discussion he agreed to exchange Meurice, the three Italians and myself, against twenty Arabs, but he refused to give up the women at all, and as I knew that poor Lanternier would not thank me for separating him from his wife and daughter I did not mention him in my letter to the general. When I had finished it the

Sultan asked me whether I would not write to my family, and perceiving my hesitation, he assured me that I might write without fear for that no one should read my letter. I accordingly put both letters into the same cover, sealed them with a huge seal, and saw the *Sultan* give them to a man from Milianah, with orders to take them straight to Algiers.

I returned to the tent in high spirits to tell Meurice what I had done; the poor fellow laughed, wept, and thanked me all at once: we talked of our country and of our friends, and promised to stand by each other in good as well as in evil fortune, for we already looked upon our deliverance as certain. We were about to lie down to sleep, full of these delightful thoughts, when we found that our rug was gone. I should have complained to Abd-el-Kader, but he was at his prayers, so we were forced to stretch ourselves on the bare ground. The cold was piercing, and in the middle of the night a violent storm came on, so that before morning we were soaked to the skin.

On the 29th, Abd-el-Kader sent Milud-Ben-Arrach with the cavalry towards Mostaganem to reconnoitre, and gave us leave to revisit the ruins of Tekedemta. Some of the workmen were carting stones to build the Casabah, others preparing clay to serve as mortar, and others again finishing the redoubt. The neighbouring tribes came every day with provisions and oxen laden with wood, and a party of Moors was sent to burn lime at the nearest spot at which it could be found, about half a day's journey from Tekedemta.

At about a hundred and fifty paces to the east of the Casabah, some soldiers were busied in clearing a very large old vaulted cistern, which Abd-el-Kader has since turned into a general ammunition store; in order to avert suspicion, he has bricked up the door and built a sort of guard-room on the top. The tools were all very bad, with the exception of a few picks and shovels that had been stolen from us. The ditch varied in breadth and depth, and the slopes were uneven; and although the redoubt stood on a declivity, there was no opening to carry off the water; the earth was only bound together with branches of gum tree and oleander, and as the winters are very severe in these mountains it is more than probable that by this time the rain has washed the slopes into the ditch and that the *Sultan's* redoubt is reduced to a heap of mud.

We saw the three Italians at work here, upon which I expostulated with the *Sultan*, and represented to him that they were sailors and not labourers, and that moreover he was not at war with the nation to which they belonged; but he replied that they must earn their food, and that he was at war with every nation, for that as he had no seaports their friendship was useless to him, and that he was the greatest and most powerful of all *Sultans*, and feared no one.

On returning to the camp we found that a party of tumblers had arrived there and were performing for the amusement of the soldiers, who watched them with great attention. But we had other diversions besides this; every evening an Arab crouching in front of Abd-el-Kader's tent, sang for hour after hour. I never could catch all the words, but the following phrases were constantly repeated to a monotonous tune—

The Sultan is great, but Mahomed is yet greater.

The Sultan is very great, he is generous, brave, and holy.

The marabouts of Mecca are very great and holy.

The Sultan has fine horses; the Sultan has many horses, and they are all excellent.

The Sultan has immense treasures and much powder.

The Arabs have fruitful plains; they have mountains covered with trees, and many rivers flow from them.

We have beautiful women.

Our horses are fleet: no other horses can keep up with them.

Our camels are very strong; we have great herds of cattle and sheep.

Our guns are very good.

We have powder—plenty of powder.

Let us pray that all Christian dogs may perish.

Plenty of powder.

The soldiers flocked round the singer and listened with deep interest to this patriotic and religious hymn.

A *marabout*, a friend of Ben Faka's, came nearly every evening to our tent, and sang for hours in the same style; but his voice was so harsh and shrill, and the burden of his song so tedious, that one of our chief annoyances was the having our ears assailed for such a length of time by his deafening psalmody.

On the 2nd of October it froze even within the tents in this mountainous region, and there was no grass left for the camels near Tekedemta; accordingly the *Sultan* sent them to the table land to the southward where there was excellent pasture. These mountains abound in game of every kind, which the soldiers caught and ate unknown to Abd-el-Kader. The market established by the *Sultan* at Tekedemta is well supplied with game, and with fish from the Ouet Mina which is full of them, and of a sort of tortoise which lives in the mud and is equally disagreeable to the taste and the smell, whereas the land tortoises, which are nearly as numerous, are delicious when properly cooked.

Abd-el-Kader carried on the works at the redoubt with great ardour; fifty workmen were constantly employed upon them. To celebrate the inauguration of the new Tekedemta, the *Sultan* had the cannon brought to the redoubt, where it was loaded with stones and fired off three times, but so unskilfully that the stones flew into the midst of the camp to the great peril both of man and beast. At each discharge the *marabouts* and the workmen cried out "The *Sultan* is great!"

Abd-el-Kader has since sent seven cannons from Mascara to Tekedemta: they were old Spanish six and eight pounders, which had all been spiked, and were mounted on very bad carriages of Arab manufacture. Fifteen or twenty families have emigrated from Mascara to Tekedemta, at the *Sultan's* command: but it will not be easy to induce the whole population of Mascara to leave their habitations and to settle in a cold, unhealthy spot to which all provisions must be fetched on mules from the distance of a day's journey, and where they consequently are very dear. Abd-el-Kader hopes to breathe new life into these remains of past greatness and splendour, but the descendants of the men who founded and built this city are unable to tell the prisoner or the traveller so much as the very name of the *Sultans* who had their capital in these mountains.

CHAPTER 8

Marches

On the 30th of September, at sunrise, Abd-el-Kader gave the signal of departure. After a march of two hours we reached a desert country; the road was extremely bad, and frequently broken by ravines. To our left ran a long chain of wooded mountains, which we had not yet left behind us, when Ben Faka ordered a halt, and pitched the camp on the banks of the Ouet Mina.

The next day, the 1st of October, whilst I was watching the negroes who were taking down the *Sultan's* tent and loading it on the mules, I saw Ben Faka with three *haicks* under his arm, followed by three Italian prisoners, I went towards them and asked whither they were going, but before they had time to answer me Ben Faka, in a voice broken by rage, commanded me to leave them, and to mount my mule. I was struck with a sinister presentiment as to the fate of the three unhappy prisoners. From afar I saw Ben Faka give them the *haicks*, of which they had long stood in need, as they had nothing to wear but their ragged shirts. My three companions in misfortune then took the road to Tekedemta.

The *Sultan* sent them to the works there, and it was only by his especial orders that Ben Faka had given them the *haicks*. At Tekedemta the poor fellows were exposed to every kind of privation and ill usage; one of them sunk under it. The two survivors afterwards gave me an account of their sufferings, which would appear incredible to anyone who did not know the Arabs as well as I do. This separation was most painful to me; we had endured together hunger, cold, insults, and blows; we had talked together of our sorrows, our hopes, and our hatred of the Arabs.

We started at daybreak, and marched eastward, still keeping the chain of mountains on our left. After a march of three hours, Ben Faka pitched the camp on the left bank of the Ouet Mina, upon a *plateau* covered with empty silos. Not a tent or even a single Arab was to be seen: the horsemen were obliged to ride for three or four hours in search of barley for their horses.

On the 4th of October we again struck our camp, and marched to within half a league of the wooded mountains I have mentioned above. Ben Faka pitched the camp on a small plain by the side of a stream which runs into the Ouet Mina. This plain is uncultivated, and in the winter it is so overflowed by the Ouet Mina as to look like a lake. It is covered with shrubs resembling the sweet briar, which bear a fruit like the medlar, only smaller, and containing a kernel. Like all the shrubs of this country, these swarm with large white snails and slugs enough to feed an army for some days. Next day we continued our march westward, bearing a few degrees to the north. We quitted the banks of the Ouet Mina, but the wooded mountain was still to our left.

After six hours' march we halted on a *plateau* covered with heaps of stones which looked like the ruins of a town: but Abd-el-Kader and his *marabouts* told us they had never heard of the existence of one on that spot.

On the 6th of October, after a march of two hours, the camp was pitched on a *plateau* at the eastern extremity of the plain of Mascara, at a place called Teknifil. Near it, on five hillocks, stand five *marabouts*. Here we heard that the French had sent an expedition from Oran, and that General Létang was marching on El-Borgj, a village two leagues to the north of Teknifil. Abd-el-Kader immediately went to El-Borgj with all his cavalry, and forced the inhabitants to abandon it. Next day the baggage, the flocks, the women, and children of the Borgia tribe were scattered about the plain, and orders were likewise sent to the inhabitants of Mascara, which is four leagues from Teknifil, to abandon the place.

We stayed at Teknifil a fortnight, during which time Abd-el-Kader gathered together all the tribes that remained faithful to him, and when his army amounted to five or six thousand he followed the French to the plains of Macta. Every day couriers arrived at the camp with false news, either that the French were surrounded on all sides, or that they had been cut to pieces by the *Sultan*. The Arabs announced the news to us, and accompanied it by blows, abuse, and menaces of death. Moreover, we were half starved, and the hopes with which Abd-el-Kader's kindness had inspired us were now turned into despair.

Our days seemed long and gloomy: the Arabs maltreated us, and separated Meurice and me from the coral fishers. We had talked so long of our hopes, our home, and our families, that these subjects were quite worn out. At last, in order to pass the time, I set to work to make a chess board and a pack of cards. I stole a board from one of the powder chests (which it was my great amusement to water, at the risk of my life), and divided it into squares: I then cut some chess men out of branches of oleander: I also stole a few sheets of paper, for which Ben Faka beat me with a stick, and made a pack of cards of them.

My knaves were jockeys with pipes in their mouths, and red, green, and white jackets; the queens were ladies dressed in the European fashion,—one with a bonnet, another with a foulard, another with hair dressed *à la Chinoise*, and the fourth with long ringlets in the English style; the kings had huge crowns on their heads. Ben Faka and Ben Abu, who had the care of Abd-el-Kader's tent during his absence, sent Meurice and me to guard it during great part of the day; for Christians and slaves as we were, they trusted us far more than the Arabs. The cushions and the sofa had been removed, and we were especially commanded to touch nothing in the tent, as the touch of a Christian would defile anything belonging to the *Sultan*. We lay on the carpet of this august and holy dwelling, and played at chess and picquet.

The *marabouts*, in spite of their horror of any representation of the human face or figure, were struck with admiration at the accuracy with which I had copied the European costume in my knaves and queens. They were very anxious to understand the game of picquet, and overpowered us with questions about every card we played. Their cards are quite different to ours, and I have seen draughts in their *cafés* but no chess boards, though one day when Abd-el-Kader saw me playing at chess with Meurice, he said, "My grandfather used sometimes to play with pieces like those on a draught board."

On the 20th of October, after a halt of fourteen days at the five *marabouts*, during which time we were exposed to threats, blows, and cruel privations, the tents were struck. A courier arrived at the camp, in the middle of the night, with the news that the French were marching towards Oran, and that the *Sultan* would be at Mascara on the morning of the 21st. In spite of the lateness of the hour (it was midnight) Ben Faka ordered the troops and the baggage to set out. There was a thick fog, and we suffered cruelly from the cold and damp, which I am sure laid the seeds of the illness under which poor Meurice finally sank. Meurice and I were mounted on the mules which carried the

Sultan's coffers. Each quarter of an hour we heard the voice of Ben Faka calling through the darkness, "France! Meurice! are you on your mules?"

"Yes."

"Don't get down, and above all don't change with any of the horsemen."

"Never fear."

Ben Faka's uneasiness was not without cause: he was responsible for any disorder that might happen during the march, and he was always afraid that if we quitted our mules the soldiers of the escort would pillage the *Sultan's* treasure; for dogs and Christians as we were, Ben Faka knew that we were more trustworthy than the proud Arab warriors. With the first rays of the sun, we arrived with all the treasure safe at the pretty town of Mascara.

The camp was pitched at the foot of the mountain which bounds the plain of Mascara on the north. A little stream, whose banks were covered with oleanders, ran through the midst of it. Mascara stands in the centre of a mountain gorge, on a steep and precipitous hill; the white and cheerful-looking houses are surrounded by a perfect grove of fig trees, and a few graceful poplars and slender minarets rise like lances among them. The view was so charming that I stole a sheet of paper and went outside the camp to sketch it. But I had scarce begun, when a mounted *chaous* rode up to me and gave me a blow with his stick. To avoid a repetition of it, I ran back to the tent with my unfinished sketch.

A courier brought the news of Abd-el-Kader's arrival at the camp, and the infantry instantly armed and went about ten minute's march towards Mascara, where it drew up in two lines. Presently the cavalry arrived at full gallop, and was drawn up by Muftar in two bodies behind the infantry. As soon as Abd-el-Kader had passed them, the last soldiers, both horse and foot, quitted the line, and ran to place themselves in two rows before his tent. As he entered it, three discharges of cannon from Mascara announced the *Sultan's* return to the neighbouring tribes. The soldiers kept up a constant firing in honour of the great victory which the *Sultan* had gained over the French.

All that day the camp was in a state of great confusion; horsemen belonging to the adjacent tribes were continually coming and going, and feeding their horses in the camp: this, added to the cries of joy and exultation, and the incessant galloping and firing of the soldiers, produced an indescribable tumult and clamour.

At sunset Abd-el-Kader mounted his horse, accompanied by a few *marabouts* and the thirty negroes, and rode to his wife's tent, which is pitched three or four miles to the south of Mascara, on a spot near which Abd-el-Kader has a garden and a *marabout*.

The chiefs who accompany the *Sultan* also have tents for their wives and families at the same place, where there is a sort of female camp. That inhabited by Abd-el-Kader's wife is woven of black camel hair.

The *Sultan* is said to be a most tender husband, and his conduct proves the truth of the report for he has not a single concubine. His wife is very pretty; her tall slender figure is seen to great advantage under the graceful folds of her *haick*, which is girded round her middle with a red worsted cord. The Arabs usually like large fat women, but Abd-el-Kader's taste is different. Though often absent from his wife for three or four months at a time, his attachment to her remains unchanged. Even from the banks of the Ouet Mina he frequently sent her presents of fruit, butter, honey, and other rarities. He has had one daughter by her; and though it was asserted that she was delivered of a boy on the very day on which the French entered Mascara, I do not believe it; for if Abd-el-Kader really had a son I am sure the Arabs would have told me so.

During the night the thirty negroes keep watch round the tent that nothing may disturb the repose of Abd-el-Kader and his wife; and during their absence from the camp, a guard of foot soldiers supplies their place around the *Sultan's* tent.

In the middle of the night a man peeped cautiously out of the *Sultan's* tent, darted out, and tried to make his escape; but the sentinels who were not asleep seized him. It was Zaka, an old negro slave, and Abd-el-Kader's cup-bearer. He had long been used to take advantage of the moments during which the *Sultan* left his tent to enter it and rob his treasure. The thirty negroes, either blinded by the confidence with which his high functions inspired him, or unwilling to denounce their comrade, had never stopped him, although they had frequently seen him leave the tent at undue hours, and during the absence of the *Sultan*. But the Arab soldiers were much less accommodating; and when Abd-el-Kader returned to the camp at sunrise they brought Zaka before him, together with several *sultani* (a silver coin) found on his person.

The coffee-sellers deposed, that Zaka had for a long time been in the habit of spending a great deal of money in their booths, and of treating his friends there daily. *Haicks, bernouses, yataghans*, and splendid pistols were found in his tent; and everyone knew that his means were small and uncertain. Abd-el-Kader ordered him to be put in irons for an unlimited time; and he was brought to our tent, and placed under the guard of his friend Ben Faka. As the punishment promised to last very long, the *chaous* struck a nail through the bar which joins the irons, instead of securing it with a padlock.

Ben Faka was presently summoned to his duties in Abd-el-Kader's tent; and after his departure Zaka crept to the further extremity of the tent, threw himself on the ground like a man overcome with fatigue, and pretended to sleep. Meurice watched all his movements with great attention, "The negro is trying to escape," said he.

"He is asleep," I replied; "besides, both his feet are hampered."

"Say rather, he is pretending to sleep," answered Meurice; "only watch his proceedings."

Zaka took down a rifle which he laid across two bales; he then pulled off his black *bernouse*, hung it over the gun, and crouched down behind it. I left the tent, and soon after saw him slowly cross the camp, wrapped in his white *haick*, and hiding his face. As soon as he had reached the limits of the camp he took to his heels, and soon disappeared among the fig trees on the mountain.

When Ben Faka returned to the tent, and found that the prisoner for whom he was personally responsible had escaped, he flew into a violent passion, and loaded us with blows and abuse, for not having prevented Zaka's flight. A hundred horsemen mounted immediately, and rode in all directions in pursuit of him. Ben Faka was anxious to conceal the escape of Zaka from the *Sultan*, as he hoped that the fugitive would be retaken before the news of his flight could reach Abd-el-Kader. But the horsemen had not returned when a *chaous* summoned him into the presence of the *Sultan*.

As Ben Faka was going towards the tent he met Zaka in the midst of an escort of horsemen, with his hands tied behind his back; he took possession of his prisoner, and went with him to the *Sultan's* tent. Without further enquiry, the *Sultan* condemned Zaka to be put in irons for an indefinite time, and to receive six hundred blows a day with a stick, for three successive days; two hundred at seven in the morning, two hundred at noon, and two hundred at night; in all one thousand eight hundred blows in three days. Zaka was instantly brought before our tent, and laid flat upon his face; two of his friends held the skirts of his *bernouse*, while the *chaous* administered to him the first two hundred blows.

The important post which Zaka had filled, joined to his munificence, had gained him many friends, to whose zeal he now entirely owed his life. He could not possibly have survived the one thousand eight hundred blows well laid on, but the *chaous* took care not to hit very hard, and the Arabs who held the skirts of his *bernouse* stretched them so tight, as considerably to deaden the force of the blows. When the *chaous* had administered the first two hundred, Zaka was brought into our tent, where his friends busied themselves in kneading and chafing his whole body, and in warming him; and Ben Faka, who now remembered nothing but his former friendship, loaded him with attentions and gave him coffee. By degrees Zaka recovered, but he was not released from his irons, and at the time of my departure he was still stretched upon the ground, vainly expecting each day the *Sultan's* order for his release.

The *Sultan* administers justice in a very simple and expeditious manner. The contending parties are brought to his tent, where the accuser first makes his complaint; the witnesses, if there be any, are then examined, after which the accused makes his defence. Both accusation and defence, like all Arab explanations, are long-winded and clamorous. When the pleadings are at an end, the *Sultan* decides singly, and without appeal. Without saying a word, he condemns the guilty to any kind of punishment by signs to the *chaous*. He raises his hand, and the accused is carried to prison; he holds it out horizontally, and the accused is led beyond the limits of the camp, and his head is cut off by the *chaous*; he bends his hand towards the earth, and the accused is dragged away and bound, laid flat upon the earth, and beaten with a stick. The *Sultan* usually determines the number of blows; if he omits to do so, it is left to the discretion of the *chaous*.

Most of the complaints and accusations are of thefts, a crime exceedingly common among the Arabs, and generally treated with great leniency, especially by Abd-el-Kader, who is neither cruel nor vindictive.

CHAPTER 9

Offers of Exchange

One evening at sunset, when Meurice and I returned to our tent, after spending the day in a garden near the camp, Ben Faka told me that the *Sultan* desired to see me. I went to his tent, where he gave me two letters, one for Meurice and the other from General Rapatel for myself. I opened the latter, and informed the *Sultan* of its contents, which were to this effect: General Rapatel offered Abd-el-Kader the choice of ten Arab prisoners, in exchange for the six Frenchmen and Italians, and ten others in exchange for Mahomed Ben Hussein, the ex-*Bey* of Medeah; adding, that the European prisoners might be sent at once to some French town, and that Abd-el-Kader should receive the Arabs in exchange for them immediately upon their return from Marseilles.

At this sentence Abd-el-Kader smiled, and said "You shall go as soon as my Arabs arrive at the camp."

The *Bey* of Medeah, who was our ally, had been taken prisoner by the *Bey* of Milianah, loaded with chains, and thrown into the dungeons of Ouchda, a town on the frontier of Morocco, where he still languishes, (as at time of first publication), exposed to the most cruel treatment, and in constant danger of being starved to death by his inhuman gaolers.

After consulting the *marabouts* who surrounded him, Abd-el-Kader ordered me to write word, that he demanded twenty prisoners in exchange for the six Europeans, and that he would give up the *Bey* of Medeah in exchange for all the prisoners at Marseilles. I remonstrated with him on the unreasonableness of his terms, and suggested that he should split the difference, and take fifteen Arabs as ransom for us. To this he agreed, and I wrote to the general and to my family. As I was sealing the letters, Abd-el-Kader said, that he hoped I had written all that I wished to say; and that I should not be deterred by fear of his displeasure from writing anything that I saw, or from expressing any opinion upon his manner of treating his prisoners; "For," said he, "a *Sultan* so great and holy as I fears no one upon earth."

I hastened to take Meurice his wife's letter, and to inform him of the favourable dispositions of Abd-el-Kader; and I had the satisfaction of seeing him fall asleep with a smile on his face. I crept close to him to warm his frozen limbs; but the night was so cold, that in the morning when we wanted to rise Meurice's legs were benumbed, and he was forced to lie upon the ground. All his blood had rushed to his head, which caused him the most violent pain. At about eleven o'clock. I carried him out into the sunshine, in hopes that the warmth might do him good.

On the 28th of October Abd-el-Kader received a letter from Morocco, announcing the death of the King of France. I believe that the Emperor of Morocco meant Charles X., but Abd-el-Kader thought it was Louis Philippe, and immediately spread a report that the King of the French had been assassinated, that a civil war had broken out in France, and that all the troops stationed at Algiers were about to be recalled.

This news excited universal joy; the troops prepared to celebrate the retreat of the French in a manner worthy of the greatness of the occasion, and three whole days were spent in festivities, both at Mascara and in the camp. These consisted chiefly in sham fights, in which the first division of cavalry, dressed in bluejackets and red trowsers, and without *haicks* or *bernouses*, represented the French, and were headed by Abd-el-Kader; the second, with their flowing *haicks* and *bernouses*, were the Arabs. The two troops were drawn up at a considerable distance from each other.

Abd-el-Kader first detached ten of his French corps as skirmishers, who were met by the same number of the opposite party. The assailants on both sides started at a foot's pace, and by degrees urged on their horses to a gallop. When they were within five-and-twenty paces of each other, they shouted "*Ah! Ah! ah!*" fired off their rifles, waved their *haicks* and *bernouses*, drew their sabres, and acted a fight hand to hand. Ten more horsemen were then detached from each troop, and galloped into the midst of the *mêlée*, whereupon the first two bands retreated to their respective posts, while the others continued the fight. Sometimes the forty horsemen kept up the struggle, until the arrival of fresh auxiliaries on one side turned the chances against the other, who then retreated at full gallop, brandishing their sabres, firing off their rifles, and uttering loud cries.

Then a pursuit was acted, till both parties had galloped enough, and returned to their stations. At one moment the confusion became excessive; the *mêlée* was thick and violent, *bernouses* fluttered, sabres flashed, and a cloud of dust concealed the combatants, whose fierce wild shouts rung in our ears. Suddenly the drums on both sides beat the recall, and the chiefs restored order; the horsemen gave a few moments of rest to their horses, and then the racing and struggling, the strange evolutions and single combats began again with as much vehemence as ever.

This military spectacle invariably terminates with the defeat of the French. When Abd-el-Kader thinks it time to put an end to the exercises, he plunges into the thick of the *mêlée*; two Arabs then seize his horse by the bridle, one on each side, and lead the *Sultan* away captive to his tent, amid shouts of triumph and enthusiasm. Abd-el-Kader, casting around him proud glances on his followers wrapt in admiration of his warlike grace, makes his horse prance and rear till it stands upright, while the *Sultan* smiles complacently, as much as to say "Am not I a horseman indeed? "

"And so you are, my fine *Sultan*," said I to myself; "but you would not be quite so cock-a-hoop on an English saddle, for all that."

On the third and last day of this warlike exhibition Ben Faka came to me with a swaggering air and said, "There has been a battle at Tlemsen; the *kalifah* has beaten the French, and taken a great number of prisoners, whom he is going to send to the *Sultan*, so you will soon have plenty of companions."

"I believe," said I, "that you are as much deceived now as you were when you told me that Ahmed Bey had taken Bona."

Meanwhile, poor Meurice got worse every day, and I spent most of my time in rubbing his aching limbs, and in endeavouring to warm his frozen legs and feet against my breast, and to relieve the burning pain in his head, by wetting my hands, and then laying them on his forehead. I was thus occupied when Ben Faka returned to the tent, and said to me with an insulting laugh, "Come and look at the Christian prisoners whom the *kiilifah* took at Tlemsen, and has sent to the *Sultan*."

I left the tent without answering Ben Faka, and saw two unfortunate soldiers, half naked, barefooted, and in a state of indescribable wretchedness, whom the *chaous* were driving along with their sticks, just as a butcher goads the tired beasts to the slaughter-house. They halted before the *Sultan's* tent, and I attempted to approach, in order to question them, but was immediately driven away by the *chaous*.

I went back to Meurice, and was telling him what had passed when Ben Faka brought the two new prisoners into our tent, and gave each of them a *haick*. I beckoned them to draw near, and asked them their names, the regiments to which they belonged, and where they came from.

"My name is Bourgeois," replied the first; "I am an old soldier in the Eleventh, and my comrade Fleury is an ex-soldier of the Sixty-Sixth; we both belong to the battalion at Tlemsen."

"Has there been a fight there then?" said I.

"None whatever. Sir. I will tell you how it was. The Bedouins had pressed hard upon the town for some time, and no provisions could be brought to market, and so you see the garrison was put upon short commons. One's appetite grows with eating, they say; but I assure you it grows much faster with an empty stomach; and one morning, when Fleury and I were more sharp set than usual, we bethought ourselves that we would go and forage like the Bedouins. There were plenty of fruit trees outside the town, and so, without more ado, we went out to make a meal off them.

"After eating our fill, we were going back to the town again; but we had reckoned without our host. The Bedouins caught us like larks in a snare; and not content with having taken us prisoners, they have given us the *strappado* the whole way. They say, to be sure, that Abd-el-Kader has given orders to take as many prisoners as possible, and not to cut their heads off, and I suppose that is the only reason why ours are still upon our shoulders; but they have treated us brutally. However, now that we are come to Abd-el-Kader's royal palace, as you may say, I hope we shall not be quite so ill-used. But, lieutenant, if you write to the governor please don't forget just to speak a word for Bourgeois and Fleury, for these quarters are not at all to our liking."

I assured my fellow-sufferers that I would not forget them; and that very evening, with Abd-el-Kader's permission, I wrote to inform General Rapatel of their arrival, and to ask for six Arab prisoners in exchange for them.

Our new companions fully sympathised in my anxiety about Meurice's health, and forgot their own sufferings to assist me in nursing him.

On the next morning Ben Faka, in the same conceited and scornful tone in which he had announced the arrival of the prisoners from Tlemsen, informed me that another prisoner was being brought before the *Sultan*.

We went outside the tent, where we saw a French prisoner led past us. He was about fifty years of age; a long beard and thick moustache of a light colour hung dirty and matted over his naked breast; a ragged shirt covered his shoulders, which, with a pair of soldiers trowser's full of holes, and a grey hat all crushed and battered, completed his costume. The blood which dropped from the wounds on his feet and legs marked his path. A noisy and cruel escort of children, which had followed him from the outskirts of the town, never ceased from tormenting him with blows, or with throwing stones: clotted black gore dropped from several deep cuts in his head. I endeavoured to get near him, for Meurice, whom we had brought out in front of the tent, had recognised M. Lanternier, but the *chaous* drove me back with their sticks, and the prisoner was hurried past us, and dragged before Abd-el-Kader, amid the acclamations of the crowd.

At the sight of this unhappy man Abd-el-Kader was touched with pity, and ordered Ben Faka to give him a *haick* and a pair of slippers, and to conduct him to our tent. But the *chaous* who had escorted him exclaimed, that the Christian dog had refused to obey their orders, and that he ought therefore to be sent to prison. In vain did the unhappy man implore Abd-el-Kader's mercy, and lament his separation from his wife and daughter in the most heart-rending words. Abd-el-Kader, unmoved by his anguish, commanded the *chaous* to take him to the prison at Mascara, but to keep him separate from the Arab prisoners, who might otherwise ill-use him.

The unfortunate man was about to renew his entreaties for mercy, but his mouth was stopped by a blow. He passed before our tent, but we were not allowed to address to him a single word of consolation. As he passed us his eyes filled with tears, and anguish and despair were painted in his countenance. He slackened his pace for a moment to look at us; but the *chaous* beat him, and the children attacked him with abuse and with stones, one of which made a deep wound in his head—the blood gushed forth in a torrent, and the poor victim staggered; but his pitiless tormentors drove him on before them. I withdrew into the tent to hide my tears, and was soon followed by the other prisoners: we all wept together.

Meurice's state became more alarming every day. Bourgeois and Fleury chafed his limbs, and laid rags soaked in cold water upon his burning temples, whilst I went to the tent of Ben Faka's coffee-maker, where I heated his slippers and some of his rags, which I placed upon his legs and feet while still hot. With inconceivable difficulty we made him some barley-water, but he drank it with disgust, because it was not sweetened. He wished to go to Mascara, to take a vapour bath, which he fancied would cure him; and I accordingly obtained an interview with Abd-el-Kader, and asked his permission to allow me to accompany him thither, which he granted for the next day. I then asked him for some sugar for Meurice, which he immediately ordered Ben Faka to give me.

Next morning Abd-el-Kader lent us one of his baggage mules and a negro called Hassan, to take Meurice to Mascara. I led the mule by the bridle, and Hassan got up behind the sick man, and supported him in his arms. We were also accompanied by the army surgeon, called Tussis, who had studied medicine at Tunis, though not to much purpose, for he was extremely ignorant.

I went into the bath with Meurice and undressed him for he was unable to move. I had intended to take a bath myself, but the dirt and stench of the place made it impossible to me. I then went to the *kait* of Mascara, and asked leave to see M. Lanternier, which the *kait* refused. On hearing my disappointment, Hassan told me that he would go and find out his prison, and conduct me to it. I returned to Meurice in the meantime, and found him in a state of perfect despair, as the Arabs had refused to shampoo him, for fear of defiling themselves by touching a Christian. Fortunately Jean Mardulin, a French deserter, came to his assistance, and shampooed him as well as he was able: he then dressed him, and wrapped him in two or three rugs, which the *Sultan* had given him for the purpose.

Meanwhile I went to fetch Tussis, who was to bleed the sick, man; but Tussis referred me to a barber, who spoke pretty good Spanish. When I had explained to him what I wanted, he took his basin and razor, a glass, fire, and paper, and followed us to the baths. He first shaved the back of Meurice's head, made several incisions in it with the razor, and then covered it with a glass, under which he placed several pieces of lighted paper. The blood flowed freely, and Meurice found himself somewhat relieved. Tussis watched his proceedings with great attention, and seemed to me to be taking a lesson in practical surgery, whilst he affected to consider the operation of too little importance for the exercise of his own skill.

We were now ordered to leave the bath, as the time appropriated to the women was come. Mardulin and I wrapped Meurice in the rugs from head to foot, and carried him to the hospital, where we left him to sleep till it was time to return to the camp. I had been very hot in the bath, and on leaving it I felt a chill. As soon as Meurice was asleep I went out into the public square, and laid myself upon the ground in the sun. Before long I saw Hassan, who beckoned to me mysteriously to follow him. We crossed the square, and stopped before a house, the door of which was open. "That," said he, "is Lanternier's prison; but take care you are not caught, or you will be beaten."

I have already said, that the door of the house was open; within it was an iron grating. At the distance of about two feet (*i. e.* The thickness of the wall) was another door, with a second iron grating, within which were crowded the Arab prisoners with no air or light but what the grating admitted. Between the two gratings, like a wild beast in a cage, was Lanternier, crouching on the ground, covered with rags, pale and emaciated. The dirt and disorder in his person, and the expression of stupid despondency in his countenance, showed what he must have endured. His eyes glared with a sort of feverish brightness.

I drew near, and told him who I was. He described to me his misfortunes, the sufferings of his wife and daughter, the ill-usage he had received from the *chaous*. He said that his prison was horrible; that it was only cleaned once a week; and that at night, when the outer door was shut, he was almost suffocated by the stench of the inner room, from which he was only separated by the grating; that he received no food but a bit of barley cake in the morning, and a handful of boiled barley at night; and that he must have died of hunger, but for the kindness of Mardulin, who brought him a bit of white bread and some snuff every morning. He implored me to intercede for him with Abd-el-Kader, that he might be allowed to go to the camp to the other Christian prisoners.

The sentinel now began to look at me suspiciously, and I departed, overwhelmed with grief. My mental sufferings, combined with the chill which had seized me on coming out of the bath made me ill, and I followed the mule, on which Hassan had placed Meurice, with tottering steps. When I awoke next morning, I was as ill as Meurice; my legs were frozen, my head ached violently, and I was unable to stand. Bourgeois was indefatigable in rendering every assistance in his power to both of us.

On the 2nd of November some Arabs brought from Mascara three of the frames upon which are stretched the *haicks* which hide the

Moorish women when they travel in panniers on the backs of mules. We heard that these were intended to conceal Lanternier's wife and daughter and the two German women, whom Abd-el-Kader was going to send as a present to Muley Abd-el-Rachman, Emperor of Morocco. These three frames were each balanced by chests, destined to contain five wild beasts, which, together with the women, some ostriches, and some carpets, constituted the *Sultan's* present to the emperor.

One morning, when Abd-el-Kader returned from his wife's tent, which he visited every night, he brought back with him Benedicto, the little Italian sailor-boy, who had been living among the women for several months. The poor child was very beautiful, and remarkably intelligent. The Arab women had been very kind to him, in spite of which he had been left without any other covering than the shirt he wore when taken prisoner. He had entirely forgotten his mother and his country, and already spoke Arabic better than Italian. When we asked him where his mother was, he pointed to the women's tents; if we enquired what was his religion, he said he was a Mahomedan; he recited the Mahomedan prayer perfectly; and the Arab soldiers, who petted him very much, often made him repeat it fifteen or twenty times in succession.

I had heard that the *Sultan* intended to remove his camp on the 26th to the neighbourhood of Tlemsen, I therefore asked leave to speak to him, and, on obtaining it, was carried into his presence. I again besought him to send Meurice to Oran, and assured him that if he did not, the unhappy man would be dead in a week. Abd-el-Kader replied with his usual smile, "If he is so ill as you say, the journey to Oran would kill him: but, instead of following my camp, you shall remain at Mascara, where you shall be lodged in a comfortable house till you can be exchanged." He then ordered Ben Faka to give each of us a *haick*, and a little vest for the child.

I returned to the tent overwhelmed with grief, and poor Meurice, who had flattered himself with the hopes of returning to Oran, read the cruel disappointment in my face, and began to bewail his misfortunes, and to inveigh against Abd-el-Kader's barbarity. I tried to comfort him with the prospect of being sheltered, warmed, and fed at Mascara, and protected against the brutality of the Arabs; but he answered, "It is all too late!" hid his head under his *haick*, and lay on the ground stupefied by misery.

CHAPTER 10

Death of Meurice

During the afternoon of the 5th a mule was brought to convey Meurice to Mascara, and I asked for another for myself; but in spite of my illness it was refused me. I revenged myself by pouring several pitchers of water into the chests containing cartridges which stood in our tent; and I flatter myself that I watered them so thoroughly as to prevent their ever being of much use to my persecutors.

I had no sooner accomplished my revenge than Ben Faka returned with the *kait* of Mascara who was to escort us to the town, and we immediately started, accompanied by Fleury, Bourgeois, and little Benedicto. I was so overpowered by illness and fatigue that at length even the *kait* took pity on me, and seeing that I was totally unable to walk, ordered Bourgeois and Fleury to lift me up on the mule behind Meurice.

The *kait* conducted us to a small house next door to that in which he administers justice, and informed us that this was to be our dwelling. It consisted of two small rooms on the ground floor, and one above which was accessible only by an external staircase in the court. We took up our quarters in the upper room, as it seemed rather less damp than the others. It was quite bare of any sort of furniture, and received a little light and a good deal of cold wind through two loopholes looking into the court. A plank about three feet wide, fixed against the wall, seemed intended to serve as a bed.

The *kait* gave us a piece of an old camel hair tent and two rugs to cover us. The two soldiers had the tent, and Meurice and I the rugs.

The *Sultan's* artillery was just passing through Mascara on its road to Tekedemta, and Jean Mardulin who belonged to it, came to visit us; he found us so ill and miserable that he proposed to stay and take care of us,—an offer which we accepted with joy and gratitude. He had scraped together a little money, which he generously placed at our disposal.

Meurice begged for an interview with Lanternier, but the *kait* replied, that he had received strict orders from Abd-el-Kader not to allow him to communicate with the other prisoners. We, however, sent him a share of our rations every day by Mardulin.

So far were we from recovering our health that I had now entirely lost the use of my legs, and my headaches daily increased in violence. I begged the *kait* twenty times to let me be bled; and at length he sent me the same barber who had operated on Meurice. The barber cupped me on the back of my head, which relieved me very much.

On the morning of the 12th the weather was detestable, the rain fell in torrents, and we suffered even more than usual from cold and damp. Meurice stretched out his hand towards me, as we lay side by side; I took it, and asked him how he felt. He replied that he was no better and felt very cold. I crept closer to him and offered him my *haick*; but he refused it, saying that he did not suffer more than the day before, but that he felt he had not long to live. "You," said he, "are young and strong; you will return to Algiers, where you will see my wife—poor Clarisse! tell her how much I loved her, and that my last thought was of her." He then covered his head with his *haick*, and for half an hour uttered not a single groan. At the end of that time I took hold of his arm and asked him how he felt: he made no answer, and I uncovered his face—he was dead.

I will not attempt to describe the feelings which crowded upon me as I lay with Meurice's body by my side. Night was come, and I called the other prisoners, and bade them examine whether our poor companion was really dead. They went to fetch the *kait*, who, now that it was too late, ordered a fire for us. Had this been granted us a few days earlier, Meurice might have been saved. Bourgeois and Mardulin undressed the body, rolled it in a rug, and laid it in the opposite corner of the room. They gave me his clothes. The vermin on the *haick* were so thick that it stood on end; but misery by degrees blunts all our sensibilities, both moral and physical. I rolled myself in his clothes, and at least was warmer.

The next afternoon Mardulin and Bourgeois, assisted by a couple of Jews, whom the *kait* had appointed for the purpose, removed the body. They dug a hole just outside the wall of the town, on the road to El Borgj, sewed the body in a ragged piece of old *haick*, and buried it there.

The weather that night was terrific; the rain fell in torrents, and the wind blew a perfect gale; nevertheless, at sunrise an Arab came to inform the *kait* that the corpse of the Christian was half out of the earth. In spite of the weather the Arabs had dug up the body, in order to steal the ragged piece of *haick* in which Mardulin had sewn it. The *kait* affected to be very angry, and promised us that he would punish the thieves; but he made no attempt to discover them. Mardulin immediately went to the spot where he had buried Meurice, enlarged the hole, and replaced in it our unfortunate companion, whom these barbarians would not suffer to rest in peace, even after death.

When Abd-el-Kader heard of Meurice's death, he sent the most positive orders that we were to have everything we might want; and the *kait* asked me what I wished for. I asked for three fowls, and for permission for Lanternier to join us. As the *kait* wished to keep me alive, I obtained both my requests. It is impossible to describe the joy of poor Lanternier, who immediately set about curing me by continued and violent friction and the application of red-hot bricks to my legs, which were so completely benumbed that even when the skin was burnt I did not feel it.

All this time the *Sultan* was encamped to the south of Oran, at a place where there are several *marabouts* and some mineral springs. He had sent Milud-ben-Arrach with the cavalry to Milianah to collect tribute from the Hadjutes of the neighbouring tribes. He was to have gone among the Hadjutes himself during the month of September, but had been prevented by the revolt of the Beni-Flitas.

I heard one day that a courier had arrived with letters from Algiers, which he had delivered to the *kait*. I got Bourgeois and Mardulin to carry me to his house, though certainly nothing of less importance would have induced me to be thus dragged across the public place of Mascara. The *kait* was touched with pity at my deplorable condition. He told me that the courier brought a letter from Algiers, which, no doubt, would effect my deliverance. I asked to see it, and my joy was inexpressible on beholding General Rapatel's seal. Guess, then, what was my disappointment when the *kait* told me that he dared not open it, but would send it at once to the *Sultan*, and that Fleury should accompany the courier in order to read it, as I was too weak and ill to bear the fatigue of the journey.

Just as the courier was about to start, four new prisoners arrived; these were Monsieur Pic a settler, his German servant formerly a *chasseur*, a *disciplinaire*, and Madame Laurent a *cantinière*. M. Pic's servant, who had received a ball in his hip, was left at Mascara, while the *kait* sent his three companions to the *Sultan* with the courier and Fleury. I especially charged the latter to ask the *Sultan* to exchange the four new prisoners against the four Arabs who were to have served as ransom for Meurice.

On the 18th thirty Beni-Amers,—men, women, and children, arrived at Mascara, loaded with chains. They had been taken on the road to Oran, whither they were going to place themselves under the protection of the French. Abd-el-Kader ordered the two chiefs to be hung as an example to others: the rest were thrown into prison.

Fleury returned to Mascara with the other prisoners and a soldier called Devienne, who had been taken by the Arabs near Tlemsen. The Arabs who escorted them told them that they must take off the *haicks* which had been given to them by the *Bey* of Milianah, and appear before the *Sultan* in their Christian dresses. The prisoners obeyed, and the *haicks* disappeared.

After questioning the prisoners, and rewarding the Arabs who had brought them, Abd-el-Kader gave each of them two bits of money, and bade them fear nothing. Fleury then read the letter in which the governor agreed to give fifteen Arabs in exchange for the six Christians, and the *Sultan* promised to send us all to Algiers at once. He also sent his command to the *kait* to clothe us all afresh with red trowsers and new *haicks*, which the latter executed as far as he was able, but the *Sultan's* store contained but one piece of cloth, which was only sufficient for three pairs of trowsers.

The *kait* promised that we should set out for Algiers as soon as the two Italian prisoners, Crescenso and Francesco, had arrived from Tekedemta, whither he had already sent to fetch them. That exchange, when we were all assembled, I begged the four new prisoners to tell us how they had fallen into the hands of the Arabs.

M. Pic and his servant were going towards Buffarik with a cartload of sand, when some Arabs rode towards them, crying "Run! run!" Thinking that the Arabs meant this as a friendly warning to them to escape from some impending danger, the servant took to his heels, and M. Pic was about to follow him when the Arabs fired at them, and wounded the servant in the hip. They then took the horse out of the cart, mounted their two prisoners upon it, and carried them to the *Bey* of Milianah.

The *disciplinaire* was returning rather drunk, from a merry-making at a blockhouse near Buffarik, when he was surprised by some Arabs, who took him to their tribe near the Queen's Tomb.[1]

Madame Laurent, in company with Madame Lafôret another *cantinière*, was going to Mahelma to see her husband, when they were seized and carried to the tents of the same tribe; where for two months they were subjected to every sort of horrible ill usage, under which they both fell sick, and Madame Lafôret soon perished.

Madame Laurent got worse and worse, and at last her master soldier to another Arab, who kept her for two months, at the end of which time, finding her as ill as ever and utterly unable to work, he took her to the *Bey* of Milianah.

The *disciplinaire* with whom on she had never been allowed to have any communication, had also fallen sick and was carried to the *Bey*.

On their arrival at Mascara, these prisoners were in the most abject state of misery and dirt. Fleury cut off Madame Laurent's long hair which was covered with vermin, and she bought a comb with the money the *Sultan* had given her. The *kait* lodged her with his women, but she soon returned to us in a rage, as the Arab women had struck and insulted her, and she was forced to take refuge from their malice with us.

Our days were passed in the following: manner. At daybreak Mardulin woke us, lighted the fire, and went to market to buy with his own savings figs, eggs, and white bread for us, and snuff for M. Lanternier. We then breakfasted; after which we cleaned the house by turns. When the weather was fine we went to sit upon the terrace of the Casabah, and hunted the vermin on our clothes: only M. Pic's servant, whose wound did not heal, stayed within.

One day, while I was discussing with Mardulin how to obtain from the French government his pardon and permission to return—a favour he so well deserved for his devotion and kindness to us, we overheard the following conversation among the other prisoners. They were talking about their return to Algiers: and in spite of their rags and vermin they had forgotten their miserable condition, and already fancied themselves free.

"I hope, gentlemen," said M. Pic "that when you pass through Buffarik on your return to Algiers, you will do me the honour of stopping to breakfast with me. Madame Pic will be extremely flattered by the compliment, and should any confusion reign in the meal, be so good, gentlemen, as not to attribute it to the slightest indifference on our part to the comfort of our guests, but to the joy which will no

---

1. *Vide* page 74 of *The Soldier in the Foreign Legion.*

doubt disturb my wife, who of course believes me to be dead, and will feel considerable emotion at our meeting."

"Gentlemen," began M. Lanternier, "I will not be outdone; you must all give me the pleasure of your company at dinner at my village of Adel-Ibrahim. It is true, I am old, but to celebrate the day of our release I will take care that not even the youngest among you shall eat and drink more than I."

"*Ah ça,*" broke in Madame Laurent; "I trust, gentlemen, that I need not put up with the disgrace of being unable to offer you any civility. But first, I wish to know if there is a carriage road from Buffarik to Algiers."

"*Petite mère,*" answered the deserter, "you shall have a car whereon to make your triumphal entry into Algiers."

"Be quiet you rogues,—I shall have the honour of receiving you at my canteen, and of offering each of you a glass of wine. The celebrated and unfortunate captives of the Bedouins shall have the privilege of drinking whatever they please gratis, like in the Champs Elysées on the birthday of Louis XVIII. I shall have the honour of waiting upon you myself, gentlemen; and I beg you to believe that my dress will be more carefully arranged and composed of better materials than it is at this present, most amiable and unfortunate captives of the barbarians."

"Long live Madame Laurent!" exclaimed all the prisoners at once; "the amiable captives will all assemble at your canteen at Algiers."

"And at night," added M. Lanternier, "we will all sup together with due honours."

"And you, *Lieutenant,*" said Madame Laurent turning to me, "will you do us the honour to be of the party?"

"Certainly, *petite mère*" replied I; "and long live Madame Laurent."

This is but one specimen of the conversations which continually arose on this subject.

After taking a few turns on the terrace we returned to our house, and as soon as the evening began to close in. Bourgeois brought the kitchen fire into our room in a chafing dish, and one of the soldiers went to fetch our supper and oil for our lamp at the house to which he was directed by one of the *kait's* slaves; for the inhabitants of the town were forced to supply us by turns: meanwhile some of the party smoked, and others played at cards or chess with those I had manufactured. When we had eaten our *kuskussu* we called on M. Lanternier for a story, and listened with the deepest interest to *Tom Thumb, Little*

Red Riding Hood, the *Sleeping Beauty in the Wood*, or some other fairy tale, which he told with great fluency and grace. The *disciplinaire*, who had a very fine voice, sang *Provençal* songs with great taste and feeling. One by one we fell asleep, and thus ended our day.

One afternoon our talk was interrupted by the noise of cannon and muskets, and of tumultuous voices. We went out to discover the cause, and were shocked at seeing the heads of fourteen slaughtered *spahis* which the children were kicking about before the door of our house. They were afterwards put into a sack and sent to adorn Abd-el-Kader's tent. This hideous spectacle made me sick.

On the 24th, two of the Italian fishermen, Crescenso and Francesco, arrived from Tekedemta: Berthoumian had died of cold and ill usage, and had been buried there. The account of their sufferings was terrible. Their first enquiry was after little Benedicto, but the boy did not remember his friends or his country; only when they mentioned his mother Maria he seemed to feel some emotion and his memory to revive. "My mother," said the boy, "is there," pointing towards the tent of Abd-el-Kader's wife; and away he ran to play with the Arab children.

CHAPTER 11

Arrival at Algiers

The next day the *kait* of Mascara announced to us that we were soon to proceed to Algiers, and that he had received orders from Abd-el-Kader to clothe us, which he accordingly did. The following morning we started amid the threats and insults of the women, children, and inhabitants of the town, and took Benedicto with us by force. The *kait* had the cruelty to send Mardulin out of the way, so that we could not press the hand of one who had been our benefactor during our stay at Mascara.

We had scarce left the town when the *kait* ordered a halt and counted us over three several times: we were twelve Christian prisoners and three deserters: four of the prisoners were compelled to walk for want of mules, but were to ride by turns with the others. Together with several Jews and Arabs who had joined our caravan, we formed a body of forty, conducted by a *kait* from the neighbourhood of Mascara, and guarded by one of Abd-el-Kader's horsemen. The *kait* then left us after having enjoined upon the chief of the escort to treat us well.

Soon after mid-day we saw the village of El-Borgj, but we made a detour to avoid it, as it was market day, and the *kait* feared we might fall victims to the hatred and fury of the assembled Arabs: is it was, the women and children came running towards us, and loaded us with threats and abuse. Towards night, after travelling over various hills, rocks and brushwood, through a savage and uncultivated country, we reached a little village at a few leagues from the falls of the Ouet Mina. The situation of this village at the foot of a mountain near several streams is delicious; rhododendrons, poplars, almond, fig, peach, and apricot trees, cover the whole plain, and the gardens are kept fresh and green by a plentiful supply of water.

After some delay we were ushered into a sort of stable, and when the *marabout* had recited a prayer some excellent *kuskussu* was brought to us. We passed a bad night owing to the smoke. On the following day, in about four hours, we reached the village of a tribe on the banks of the Ouet Mina, where we procured some food: we then continued our journey towards the Schellif, avoiding the mountains inhabited by the Beni-Flitas who had shaken off Abd-el-Kader's authority. After several days' forced march over a rough country, the tired mules stumbling at every step and the men on foot suffering acutely, we reached a small village governed by an Aga of the plain of Milianah: we entered a large house in the public square, the inside of which was one vast hall, evidently intended for the reception of travellers.

At one end mats were spread on the ground for our accommodation, at the other several Arabs sitting cross-legged on rich carpets were preparing coffee. Presently the slaves brought in some splendid cushions and a handsome divan, more magnificent than those belonging to Abd-el-Kader. The Aga, sumptuously dressed, entered, accompanied by our *kait*, the young *marabout*, and several chiefs, and they began to drink coffee and smoke long pipes.

I went towards him and said that I was ill, and also a woman who was with us, and begged him to give us some coffee; upon which he not only ordered his slaves to bring us two cups, but sent Madame Laurent and Benedicto to his wife, who treated them with the utmost kindness.

The hall which we occupied presented a most picturesque and striking scene. In one corner were the Christian prisoners sitting round a large fire, talking over their miseries and their sufferings, their livid faces plainly telling the torments they had endured: many more occupied in dressing their wounds and sores; occasionally plaintive murmurs and confused groans were audible from among them. A few paces from us, on gorgeous silken cushions, the Arabs reclined in a circle round the *aga*, who looked like a *Sultan* in his splendid dress: these were drinking coffee and smoking. The flickering light made their pale faces look fiercer and wilder than usual. They were discussing the projects of Abd-el-Kader, and occasionally, when the conversation turned upon the Christians, their eyes flashed, rage deformed their countenances, and one might fancy that one saw before one some of those nomad tribes who in former ages overran Christian Europe, defiling the churches and monasteries by planting the crescent on their steeples and towers.

At the hour of prayer the young *marabout* rose and recited it: the Arabs listened with deep devotion; and from my corner I gazed upon the strange and imposing scene. We then had some *kuskussu* and half a roasted sheep.

This delicious repast and a good night's rest greatly restored our exhausted frames, and we quitted with regret a village at which we had been so hospitably treated. Next day we reached Milianah. We received the usual treatment from the Arab populace, but were at length safely lodged in the house in which the *Bey* delivers judgment. The house consisted of three small rooms on the ground floor: in one of these the slaves prepared the *Bey's* coffee; the second served as a prison for those Arabs who had taken arms for the French, some of whom were in irons, and others confined in circular blocks of wood which prevented them even from rising; the third room, which was dark, cold, and damp, was our prison. Our food was bad, and we suffered much from the exposure to damp and cold. Bourgeois, who until now had been in good health, fell ill, and our days were passed in rubbing him. The long journey too had irritated the wound of M. Pic's servant, which began to be most offensive.

We had been assured that we should start for Algiers after three days' stay at Milianah, and this had kept us from giving way to despondency. But when the time fixed for our departure went by, the future appeared to us in the most gloomy colours, despair seized upon our minds, and disease and misery wasted our bodies.

The *kait* affected not to understand Abd-el-Kader's directions, and ordered me to write to Algiers to announce the death of Meurice and Berthoumian, and that two other Christian prisoners would be liberated in their stead. These delays drove us to despair, and we looked forward with impatience to the arrival of the *Bey* of Milianah, who might perhaps hasten our deliverance: but, he never came.

In the midst of these torments we one day received the visit of a deserter, whose life and position among the Arabs are too curious to be passed over.

I had seen this man before, but have delayed until now to mention him, in order to present this episode as a whole. While Abd-el-Kader was encamped on the borders of the Ouet Mina, a handsome man, dressed in the uniform of the *spahis*, and without a *bernouse*, passed our tent, making his horse prance. The Arabs pointed him out to us, saying, "He is a Christian."

Shortly afterwards a negro came and told us that Moussa, the

Christian, desired to speak with us. As we did not wish to have any dealings with deserters we told the negro that if Moussa wished to speak with us he must come here, as we were not free to go where we liked.

Scarce had the negro left us, when a tall man with a long flowing beard and an insolent bearing came to us, saying, "I am amazed that dogs of Christians such as you refuse to come when one so great and powerful as Moulin sends for you. Has not my fame reached you; and know you not that your fate is in my hands?" On my assuring him that I did not know him, he replied, "I am Moulin: four years ago I quitted the French, and I now command the armies of the *Sultan*. It is I who lead them to victory and carry terror and destruction into the ranks of the Christian dogs. I am he who returns from every battle with the heads of four Frenchmen whom I have killed with my own hand hanging at my saddle-bow."

"My dear Sir," replied I, "you must imagine, to judge by your style of conversation, that you are talking to idiots."

"What do you say, you wretch?"

"I say that our soldiers still believe in the existence of Moulin whose name even now inspires them with terror, for after an infamous desertion he was distinguished for courage. But he has been dead for years, and we do not believe in ghosts."

"I tell you, dog of a Christian, that I am Moulin; I have taken the name of Moussa since I have become one of the faithful, and my power and authority know no bounds. I am now going to the tent of my friend Abd-el-Kader to determine your fate."

While this conversation was going on my poor friend Meurice, who was then alive, told me that he had attentively observed the deserter's features, and that they were familiar to him at Paris. He begged me next time he came to turn the conversation to Paris, in order that he might observe the impression this produced.

Next day Moussa presented himself with the same presumptuous assurance; and after a great deal of vapouring on his part I asked him if he still persisted in passing for Moulin. "Dog of a Christian, you are most obstinate. Have not the French soldiers after a battle related that the Arab battalions were commanded by the terrible Moulin?"

We then began to talk about Paris, in praise of which Moussa was most eloquent. "Do I know Paris?" cried he; "it is the place where I was born: and the theatres! I went to them every night, more especially to the Odeon."

"The Odeon!" said Meurice, with more heat than I had ever seen him exhibit. "The Odeon! You are an impostor; you are neither Moulin nor Moussa, but M——. I know you well. You used to come every evening to the director's box at the Odeon: many's the time you have sat on my knee as a child, and your sister was then a charming actress. My name, Sir, is Meurice."

Moussa was struck dumb at this vehement apostrophe, and Meurice continued, "I have never seen you since, but I have heard of you; you grew up a good-for-nothing fellow, and entered first the cavalry and then the infantry: in each your restless temper drew upon you the reprimands of your superiors; till at length you engaged in the *Bataillon d'Afrique*, and then in the *spahis*, whose uniform you still wear. I heard of your desertion in the prisons of Mascara. You may call yourself Moussa, but your name before your infamous apostasy was the one I pronounced: I do not repeat it out of regard to your family."

"I can deny nothing, Sir," said Moussa, with despair painted in his face. "I am miserable; but believe me that it was only the vexations I endured which determined me to desert. I long resisted the unfortunate idea, but I could not bend to injustice; and if I have done amiss I now expiate my faults most cruelly."

We talked in this strain for some time, and Moussa appeared truly penitent, insomuch that we forgot his crimes and his impudence in our interest in his regrets and sufferings. From this time forward I did not see him again, as Abd-el-Kader presented him with a horse, a sabre, and a rifle, and sent him to the Hadjutes, among whom he had lived since his desertion.

One day during my captivity at Mascara, Moussa came to visit me. I felt some pleasure at seeing him, and told him how miserable we were. He promised to do everything in his power, telling me that he commanded the cavalry of the Hadjutes, and that he was then on his way to Abd-el-Kader, whom he would press on the subject of our exchange. He added that he had saved some money, and hoped to escape to the coast of Spain. Meanwhile he sent me some bread and a shirt, which I accepted, as I imagined that he was still repentant. It so happened that during his absence a Hadjute had told me that he himself had, in the affair of the 3rd November, cut off the heads of three French officers of the *spahis*, which I must have seen at Mascara.

At this moment Moussa came to take leave of us, saying he had been able to do but little for us, but that on his return he would give us everything we could desire, as Abd-el-Kader would pay him handsomely for the three French officers whom he had killed, and whose heads he had sent him, adding that we should hear of him at Algiers, as he had written his name with the point of his sword on the back of one of the officers whose head he had cut off.

We could not restrain our indignation on hearing this wretch invent lie after lie, and boast of the mischief he had done to our countrymen. After loading him with opprobrious epithets, we called back the Hadjute, and told him that Moussa boasted of having cut off those very heads which he, the Hadjute, claimed as his prize. "What!" exclaimed the Hadjute; "you say you have cut off the heads of the three officers? Moussa, you lie in your throat. You cut off the heads of Christians; you are a coward and a braggart. You fled when we encountered the Christians. You fled, dog that you are, although before the battle you boasted of your courage and prowess: you are a thief and a rascal."

Then turning to us, he said—"What! did he say he was going to the *Sultan*, to his friend Abd-el-Kader? His friend, indeed! The *Sultan* has sent for him, not to load him with favours, but to call him to account for the horse, the rifle, and the *bernouse* which he gave him, and which this fellow sold at Blidah, and then got drunk with the money."

"Sooner or later I will have my revenge," said Moussa, as we forced him out of our prison. A few minutes afterwards a negro brought me a letter from Moussa to the following effect:—

As I do not choose that a dog of a Christian, such as you, should keep anything that once belonged to so great and powerful a Mussulman as myself, I herewith command you to return by the bearer the shirt which I gave you yesterday. I am going to my friend Abd-el-Kader, and shall do my best to have your head cut off. At any rate, if I arrive too late to prevent your being exchanged, you will never see your friends, as I have given orders to have you all seized as soon as you have passed Buffarik.

Upon which I give you my word of honour.

Moussa,
Commander in-Chief of the *Sultan's* armies.'

This letter excited the laughter of my companions, and we burnt the shirt which the rascal demanded in such insolent and haughty terms.

We never saw the rogue again, but heard that the *Bey* of Milianah had sent him to Abd-el-Kader, under the guard of two soldiers, charged with several offences, and with having sold the horse, the *bernouse*, and the rifle, which had been given him by the *Sultan*, who, doubtless, condemned him to that death he so richly deserved for his various crimes.

The fast of *Rhamadan* at length induced the *Bey* to return to Milianah; but his presence brought no alleviation to our sufferings. Our jailer made the fast a pretext for depriving us of our daily allowance of boiled barley, and giving us nothing but half a barley cake each. The weather continued bitterly cold, with continual snow and sleet; and our dungeon was so dark that we were unable even to catch the vermin that infested it. We at length grew quite desperate, and most of us felt convinced that the *Sultan* had sent us to die of cold and hunger in the prisons of Milianah, and that he had never intended to release or exchange us. Fleury, Bourgeois, Crescenso, M. Lanternier, and the German servant, lay on the cold bare earth sick of the fever, and their groans and delirious ravings sounded most horrible in the darkness of our dungeon.

One morning a canopy was raised in front of our prison: magnificent carpets were spread, upon which were laid cushions covered with gorgeous brocade; and before long the *Bey* came and seated himself upon them, in order to distribute the pay to his soldiers. Some slaves spread a large round skin of morocco leather at his feet, and emptied several bags of money upon it, after which the soldiers were called up by name, and each in succession received his pay.

Mahadin-el-Hadj-el-Schir-ben-Moubarek *Bey* of Milianah, is a man of about forty. He is taller than Abd-el-Kader; his face is long, his eyes small, his lips thick, and his beard grizzled. He wore a *haick*, and a *bernouse* of beautiful crimson and azure cloth, embroidered with silk and gold, and ornamented with gold tassels. A superb *yataghan* glittered at his side. His officers, who stood in a row on either side of him, were all dressed in red vests and trowsers and white *bernouses*.

When I perceived that the *Bey* did not cast a single glance upon our prison, and appeared to have forgotten our very existence, I came before him, with General Rapatel's letters in my hand, and represented to him the misery we endured, and how opposed his cruel treatment of us was to Abd-el-Kader's generous intentions. The *Bey* answered me with plenty of fine promises: he then departed, and we heard no more of him. At length a Hadjute came to announce that we were to start for the place at which the prisoners were to be exchanged, and in less than half an hour the list of names of those selected to leave Milianah that very day was brought to us. It included Madame Laurent, M. Lanternier, Crescenso, Francesco, Benedicto, and myself.

The weather was terrible; a thick snow was continually falling. M. Lanternier was so ill that he was unable even to stand, and must infallibly have dropped dead from his mule in a few hours. We therefore resolved to leave him, and to take M. Pic's German servant instead, who, though exceedingly ill from the effects of his wound, was able to sit upon his mule. We started amid the groans and lamentations of our fellow-prisoners, and the frantic complaints of Lanternier.

A few days after our departure M. Lanternier sunk under his illness, and was buried outside the gates of Milianah.

We stopped before the palace of the *Bey*, who was sitting in the court. He called me to him, and desired me to press General Rapatel to hasten the exchange of the other prisoners at the rate of three Arabs for every Christian. "If," said he, "these terms are complied with, I will leave your outposts alone for a time; if not, my Hadjutes and I will not suffer them to rest in peace a single day."

Madame Laurent and Benedicto were waiting for us before the *Bey's* palace: their condition had been very different from ours. They told us that the *Bey* had two charming daughters, whose kindness was equal to their beauty, and who had never ceased from paying them every sort of attention. At Madame Laurent's request these amiable girls had frequently sent us provisions, but the slaves who were ordered to take them to us had eaten them themselves. We all mounted our mules except Crescenso, who was obliged to follow on foot, and we quitted the town amidst the jeers and yells of the populace, who shouted after us "There go the Christian dogs."

At length we were on our way towards home: the day of our release drew near; but this moment to which we had looked forward with so much impatience failed to excite in us the joy we had expected to feel. Sickness and misery had so completely exhausted our strength and spirits, that we could think of nothing but the sufferings and fatigue of the present moment. We travelled the whole of the day over mountains covered with ilexes, gum trees, and cypresses; the roads were detestable, and it never ceased from snowing. We made no halt until evening, when we arrived at a tribe in the mountains to the west of the plain of the Metidja.

The commander of our escort, one of the officers of the *Bey* of

Milianah, conducted us to a mud hovel. A large fire was lighted, at which we dried our clothes, which were completely wetted by the snow. The Arabs of the surrounding tribes crowded to look at us, and to torment us with blows and abuse. They forced little Benedicto to repeat the Mahomedan prayer to every newcomer, and the poor child had to say it at least two hundred times that night: they then commanded us to do the same, and beat us violently when we refused.

The poor German, whose wound was gangrened, suffered most from the inhumanity of these people who kicked and struck him on his wound. We dared not remonstrate against the wanton cruelty of these Arabs, who would have been too glad of a pretext to kill us all on the spot. After torturing us for about four hours they left us, and some detestable *kuskussu* was brought for our supper. I asked for some butter and honey to dress the poor German's wounds, but it was refused. We lay down and endeavoured to sleep, but found it impossible; and Francesco and I lay concerting plans of revenge upon the Arab prisoners at Marseilles, and lamenting the hard fate of the companions we had lost.

We left this inhospitable tribe before daybreak without breakfasting, on account of the *Rhamadan*. By eleven o'clock we had reached the plain of the Metidja, and our guide pointed out to us on the horizon the position of Algiers. This sight inspired me with fresh courage. I gave up my mule to Crescenso, who was weary with walking, and my *haick* to Francesco.

The plain of the Metidja was covered with water; in many places it was up to our knees. My slippers were in a very bad state, and I soon left them sticking in the mud, and had to continue my journey barefooted. After a march of two hours we arrived at Blidah; our leader made us halt at the gates of the town, while he went to fetch the *hakem*, a governor appointed by the French, but the *hakem* was gone to Buffarik, to see whether the Arab prisoners who were to be exchanged for us had arrived, and the inhabitants of the town not only refused to allow us to enter it, but drove us away with blows and abuse; and the *kait* of the Hadjutes sent us to the tribe of the Beni-Messaons, halfway up the Atlas, where we remained two days exposed to every sort of ill-treatment.

At the end of that time we were brought back to Blidah in perfect despair; we found that the; *hakem* had returned from Buffarik, and he received us with great hospitality. Madame Laurent and Benedicto were lodged with the *hakem's* wives; the other prisoners remained in the room in which we had been received at first, and the *hakem* .sent a *chaous* to invite me to sup with him. The cookery was very different from that in Abd-el-Kader's camp, and for the first time I discovered that many of the Arab dishes, when well prepared, are excellent.

After supper the *hakem* retired, leaving the *kait* of the Hadjutes and myself to sleep in the room where we had supped. I rolled myself in a rug and was fast asleep in a moment, but I was presently awakened by the *kait*, who came and seated himself by my side, and tried to persuade me to desert my country and to remain with him. He offered me the usual inducements of fine horses, beautiful women, rich clothes, and splendid arms, and above all, plenty of powder. I was too tired to answer him anything but "Goodnight: do let me sleep."

At eight o'clock next morning the *hakem* came in and asked me whether I was satisfied with his reception. On my answering in the affirmative, he eagerly pressed me to persuade the governor to raise his salary.

Three mules were prepared for Madame Laurent, the German, and Francesco, with Benedicto behind him: Crescenso and I followed on foot. This last journey was as fatiguing and painful as any previous one; it rained the whole day, and Benedicto cried with cold. As for us, the outposts of Buffarik were before us, and we felt nothing but joy.

I will not attempt to describe the reception I met with from my brother officers, nor my subsequent illness, nor how delightful it was to be nursed by my countrymen. Francesco, Madame Laurent, the German, and Crescenso were sent to the hospital at Algiers, where they lay ill for some time. The other prisoners were soon released, except the wife and daughter of M. Lanternier, and the two German women who are still in the possession of the Emperor of Morocco. I obtained Mardulin's pardon, and contrived to communicate it to him: he escaped from Mascara with some orange merchants of Blidah, and is now enrolled among the *spahis*.

As I was on the point of embarking for France I heard myself greeted on the quay, and on turning round I saw Benedicto dressed in a new suit of clothes. "Where are you going, Benedicto?" said I.

"To my mother Maria, who has sent me these fine clothes; I am going on board with Francesco and Crescenso to sail to Genoa, where she is waiting for me."

On arriving at Marseilles, I hastened to visit the Arab prisoners, with the full intention of repaying them some of the cruelty I had endured from their countrymen. I however confined my revenge to inviting two of them to dinner: one, who was a *marabout*, would not eat, because of the *Rhamadan* but the other ate and drank wine and brandy like any Christian. He pressed me to return to his country, where he promised to give me quantities of horses and sheep, to receive me into his tent as his guest, and to watch over me while I slept. After dinner I took him to the theatre, and ended by conducting him home to his barracks and helping him to bed, for he had transgressed the law of the Prophet, and was drunk.

9 780857 067388